Organo Gold: King of Coffee
or
International Business Sensation?

Turning beverages into a Health
and Wellness Business Engine

Brian Kelly

Organo Gold: King of Coffee or International Business
Sensation?

ISBN 1492104515

The Wellness Industry – The Biggest Sandbox in the World

The term wellness is really an all-encompassing term, meaning "the quality or state of being healthy in body and mind, especially as the result of deliberate effort." It can also mean "an approach to healthcare that emphasizes preventing illness and prolonging life, as opposed to emphasizing treating diseases." As such, the wellness industry, under which Organo Gold has found such success, is also one of the largest in the world today, and for good reason. Since the beginning of time, people have always been in search of eternal youth. Nothing has changed in the thousands of years since the dawn of existence, except that modern science and research has helped identify many ways to do so.

Especially now, the wellness industry is one of the most profitable on the planet, which is due in part to the fact that the world's population is aging, especially in the United States where the Baby Boomer generation is reaching senior citizenship. Getting up there in age doesn't mean people want to start acting older, hence the age old problem of trying to find eternal youth, or at the very least, to continue feeling as good as possible for as long as possible. Growing old and feeling young and fit are not mutually exclusive, and people in the wellness industry know that. Of over 78 million aging Baby Boomers, over ten thousand will turn 50 every day for the next fifteen years. This demographic has significant spending power, more leisure time, and a vested interest in living more healthy lifestyles, all of which paint a picture for the continued growth of the wellness industry.

In addition, the cost of health care is rising and this is largely due to the high populations of people who are suffering from some sort of disease. While many of these diseases such as cardiovascular do have genetic components, a large majority of them are due to lifestyle factors, as well. It's a well-researched fact that people who are active and eat a healthy diet are at lower risk of disease than their peers who lead less healthy lifestyles.

For those considering harnessing themselves to a powerful and exploding industry, the wellness industry is arguably the best. Let's explore this industry briefly, both externally and internally before exploring Organo Gold. For examining the success of Organo Gold without understanding the wellness industry is like trying to figure out the success of Apple, Microsoft or Dell without understanding the microprocessor revolution or establishment and growth of the Internet.

I don't know where to begin. Organo Gold gave me back my strength and my life! Prior to discovering Organo, I suffered from major anxiety that caused my digestive system to stop working. All the doctors only wanted me to drink broth. Then I found that my kidney was partially shutting down. I was getting panic attacks sometimes two and three times a day! My skin turned yellow I lost all energy. I just wanted to stay in bed PLUS I gained over 40 lbs. I was miserable! I hated life. I didn't want to be seen in public.

I didn't want to hang with my friends. All I did was hold myself prisoner in my home for almost a year only doing bare minimum. Still, the saddest thing was I was sad for my sons because I didn't feel like I could stay positive for them, even though I was fighting every day just to breathe. I got diagnosed with a breathing pattern disorder. I was worried that I was setting an example of giving up and being lazy. When in reality I hadn't stop fighting I just didn't know what to equip myself with to defend myself. I was embarrassed for them because they had to see me like this, I became so angry because I thought I was losing my mind, I thought I was being weak minded. I thought it was all in my head! I couldn't control my emotions and I was trying to cover my pain. I felt like I had just jumped into a pool and was fighting to swim to the top for oxygen and I couldn't get there. After 6 doctors and no reason for any of this the consensus was I suffered from extreme negative emotions from my past that I had pushed so far deep into myself consciences that I couldn't even remember it.

Then came Organo Gold. Thanks to the wonderful products – and I take ALL of them - it helped the issues that were visible, I am breathing normally and I have lost 15 lbs., and still losing more. My skin is back to its normal color, and I have no more rashes or itching – in short - and I am living again.

Jami M. South Florida

Table of Contents

Chapter 1 The Wellness Industry – Working from the Outside In

Of course you've noticed the boom of the fitness industry, which is considered an external component of the wellness industry overall. This is due to the overwhelming scientific evidence that says exercise leads to a multitude of health benefits.

These benefits include helping protect you from developing heart disease and stroke or its precursors, which include high blood pressure and negative blood lipid patterns. Exercise also helps protect you from developing certain cancers, including colon and breast cancer, and helps prevent type 2 diabetes and metabolic syndrome. More benefits are helping prevent loss of bone known as osteoporosis, preventing weight gain, promoting weight loss, and helping keep weight off after initial weight loss. Aside from the physical benefits, exercise also has mental health benefits such as relieving symptoms of depression and anxiety and improving mood.

As mentioned, the United States, in particular, has an aging population and exercising Improves chances of living longer and living healthier, in addition to reducing the risk of falling and improving cognitive function among older adults. This makes the physical activity aspect of fitness particularly important for older individuals.

According to the American College of Sports Medicine (ACSM) it's recommended that all adults get at least 150 minutes of moderate-intensity exercise each week. This is to be beyond activities of daily living and is essential for adults. While this recommendation refers to cardiorespiratory exercise, specifically, it is also recommended that adult's resistance train each major muscle group two or three days each week using a variety of exercises and also do the same amount of flexibility exercises. In addition, functional training should be done the same number of days per week, though you should keep in mind that there is a good deal of overlap between these categories, so they don't all need to be done separately.

Given that exercising has so many benefits, it's no wonder that it's such an important aspect of the wellness industry. It's also an incredibly profitable portion of the overall industry, growing during the past couple decades. U.S. health club industry revenue reached $21.4 billion in 2011, according to the International Health, Racquet & Sports club Association (IHRSA).

Even outside of health clubs, the United States consumer fitness equipment market is already a $3.2 billion industry and experiencing a movement toward higher participation in non-traditional fitness and training regimes.

My son and I had H1N1 swine flu.   All we did was drank the Gourmet Black coffee for 3 days.   No medicine expect a few Tylenol, and then the Flu was no longer with us... Doctors were baffled.

Akeem, Kentucky

NO MORE PMS

I have been drinking Organo Gold coffee and tea since Sept 16th, 2009 and thoroughly enjoying the taste. I have struggled with my menstrual cycle ever since it began. I have never been able to menstruate drug-free before in my life. After drinking the coffee for a month, I noticed I had no PMS symptoms and had an almost pain free period. Before my period would have been a 10/10 on the pain scale, this month it was a 1/10...amazing. I have been seeking relief for these symptoms for years but to no avail. This is a miracle in my life. I wanted to share.

Thank you so much,

Andrea S. Regina, SK, Canada

Another external component of the wellness industry is the skincare industry. In addition to wanting to feel younger and have youthful looking bodies, the population is concerned with having skin to match. It's known that age plays a major role in skin health and that choices made decades ago come back to bite people in their older age. For example, time spent sun tanning or just out in the sun without sunscreen, leading to burns, can result in leathery, wrinkly, or spotty skin as a person ages. While nowadays everyone knows the benefits of protecting their skin from the sun, those things weren't known a few decades ago. And even with the knowledge, it can be hard to be motivated to reapply sun lotion all day long to prevent wrinkles in 50 years. People respond well to immediate consequences, and as such, many continue to ignore the warnings associated with unprotected time in the sun.

Due to the effects of aging on the skin, the skincare industry is another multibillion dollar industry, making up about $20 billion of the $80 billion anti-aging industry. With over 70 million Baby Boomers wanting to slow the aging process, there is no shortage in customers who are willing to pay good money for a product that promises to slow or reverse the signs of aging. Skin care remains the most important category in the global beauty market, accounting for 23% value share of total sales.

Female baby boomers are the largest personal care buying segment, known for their spending power, proactive health habits and dedication to product research. These women average 13+ hours online every week making the online market a powerful resource. While many people are inclined to turn to cosmetic surgeries for their skin concerns, these procedures are costly and sometimes risky and many people aren't willing to undergo them for the promised benefits. As a result, products like anti-aging lotions have hit the market in full force. Most of these products use active ingredients such as vitamins C, E, and derivatives of A. Other ingredients are Hydroquinone, Alpha Hydroxy Acids, Salicylic Acid, green tea, peptides, and soy. While prescription skincare products are a multibillion dollar industry on their own, a growing percentage of the population is increasingly concerned about utilizing as natural products as possible. These people are willing to pay even more money for a product that uses natural ingredients like the aforementioned soy and green tea. This is a major selling point for many people, as they'd rather be applying something that comes from the Earth to their skin than some ingredient that they can't name and was likely made in a lab.

Just as many people are growing reluctant to ingest foods that are unnatural and inorganically produced, the same rules apply to products they're placing on their skin. Part of the aging process is realizing mortality and making the connection between actions and consequences. With millions of people suffering from cancer, many of which are the result of a combination of external factors and decisions made earlier in life, older people begin to realize that their decisions have consequences. Rather than use a prescription cream made in a lab, they'd prefer to use a more natural source to do the same, as these generally have fewer harmful or unpleasant side effects.

As indicated by these enormous numbers, the wellness industry is holding strong and isn't going anywhere anytime soon. And exercise and skincare are just a portion of the industry overall. When you factor in a healthy diet, nutritional supplements, you're looking at an even larger part of the market share and even more billions of dollars.

Chapter 2 The Wellness Industry — Working from the Inside Out

As mentioned, the wellness industry can be divided into external and internal components. Previously discussed exercise and skincare industries are considered external and to-be discussed factions like diet and nutritional supplements are internal. We'll discuss a healthy diet first and then get into supplementation.

Sales of natural and organic food and beverages have been on the rise for nearly 10 years, with United States consumer sales reaching $37.4 billion. Over the last two decades, sales of organic food and beverages have grown from $1 billion to $24.8 billion. A recent trend report showed that 65% of consumers express the most desire for foods with organic ingredients and 61% of Americans have visited a natural foods store in the past year. What these statistics show is the willingness of the American people to spend top dollar to make sure they're ingesting the healthiest foods available. It's long been proven that diet plays a major role not just in overall health and wellbeing, but also reaching and maintaining a healthy weight and preventing disease onset. Daily recommendations from the USDA suggest eating nine servings of fruits and vegetables for optimal health.

My name is Sandy P. and I just wanted to let you know what the Organo Gold healthy coffee has done for my family and me. First of all, I was very skeptical...I thought it was just another scheme...not so. I was suffering from extreme joint pain I could barely lift my arms and chronic fatigue. I would come home from work and get on the couch and not be able to move...my kids quite often had to fend for dinner themselves. A friend suggested

I drink Organo Gold coffee...I usually only drank one cup of regular coffee a day, because I got the jitters and burning stomach from it if I had any more. I switched to 1 cup of the Organo Gold healthy coffee, it took me a couple of cups to get used to the different flavor, but I did like it and noticed my energy level went up a bit. I still had the joint pain. My friend suggested that I start taking the capsules...I started with 1 spore cap a day and noticed a difference in both my energy level and the joint pain. My shoulders were feeling much better!

I now drink 1-3 cups of coffee and tea a day because I love the taste and I take all the capsules because it makes me feel great...I have all the energy in the world now I am working out again and NO more joint pain. Another difference I have noticed since being on the Organo Gold products is that I don't have any 'plumbing' issues anymore. What a relief that is.

I have since got my whole family on the coffee, tea and capsules...everyone feels great and no more seasonal colds and flu.

Sandy P. Brentwood Bay

In addition, recent years have shown an increased interest in organic foods that have been untouched by hormones, antibiotics (in the case of meats), and pesticides. Studies have shown links between these chemicals and an increased risk of diseases like cancer, so it makes sense that people are cautious about what they're putting into their bodies. The more natural the ingredients, the better, which goes hand in hand with people's preferences with skincare creams, as well. People like to recognize the names of things they're putting on and in their bodies and are willing to pay top dollar to do so.

As mentioned, the aging Baby Boomer population is reaching the age of retirement and with it comes ample time to attend farmer's markets and cook healthy meals, as well as the financial means to do so.

Unfortunately, it can be very challenging to get all the necessary nutrients, vitamins, and minerals through food alone. Many micronutrients are only needed in small amounts and are not found in foods that are local to many people. As a result, the nutritional supplement industry has grown immensely in recent years.

While some people only take supplements to make sure they're getting the recommended daily amount of a certain vitamin or mineral, others supplement for a variety of other reasons, but the fact remains that more than 87% of U.S. consumers take some form of a dietary supplement. Multivitamins, which ensure a person gets the Recommended Daily Allowance of all essential vitamins and minerals make up $110 million in sales each year. Regardless of reasons for taking nutritional supplements, it remains a fact that in a single year, United States consumer sales of nutrition products grew to $108.3 billion, with supplements alone making up $26.9 billion of that. And despite tough economic times, nutrition product sales continue to grow.

In addition, sales of herbal supplements make up nearly $900 million, which represents over 17% of the total $5 billion consumer sales. Obviously these are huge amounts of money and indicate just how willing the American people are to spend their hard earned money on nutritional supplements, especially those of the herbal and natural variety.

As discussed in the first chapter, millions of people are making their health a priority, which includes regular exercise. But it's no secret that over the past thirty years prevalence of obesity in the U.S. has tripled. Nearly three-quarters of the U.S. population is overweight, obese, or extremely obese. Clearly people are not happy with being overweight and the weight loss and diet control falls under the wellness umbrella, as well. This aspect of the industry brings in approximately $60 billion in a single year. Over 69% of Americans used some form of complementary and/or alternative medicine in the last year.

As obesity accounts for around $168 billion annually in direct costs, making up nearly 17% of U.S. medical costs, it's no wonder that people are trying to get their weights under control. Not just for the physical or mental health benefits, but for the financial savings, as well.

Approximately 70% of American adults are concerned about their weight and more than half are actively trying to lose weight. Given that the effects of being obese will cost a person thousands of dollars over time, it's no wonder that so many people are willing to pay top dollar for diet and weight loss related products.

As the above information should indicate quite clearly, the wellness industry is a growing market sector and one very worthy of your attention. While the industry is really an umbrella for many other industries, they all have important aspects in common. To-gether they show the importance to the American people of youthfulness and attempts to get healthy. They show an increas-ingly fat population that is willing to spend billions of dollars to try to turn that statistic around. They show an aging population that has the time and resources to do ample research into the prod-ucts they're purchasing and the money to buy the best products on the market. They show an increased interest in natural and holistic products that won't have the harmful or adverse side ef-fects of many pharmaceutically created products.

I was skeptical at first when I heard about a healthy coffee. Could it really taste good and be good for you? As I poured the contents into the cup and mixed it with hot water, it looked and smelled like a regular cup of coffee. When I took the first sip, I thought to my-self, this isn't bad. Sip after sip, I was actually enjoying my coffee. And when I thought of the Ganoderma herb being in it, I felt even better knowing that this cup of coffee was not bad for me. After getting home, I did not feel sleepy, tired or that crashing sensation like before. For example, it is 1 a.m. and here I am typing my testimonial full of energy. Even better was the taste itself. I didn't have to add cream or sugar to it. It is delicious just like it is. I can't wait to drink another cup of Organo Gold Coffee!

Fernando C.

Organo Gold's Secret Business Formula

Lastly, they show an immense opportunity for money to be made in this sector of the market. With no shortage of promising ingredients, products, and services, it takes only a little initiative to tap into this industry and make great money while also helping people reach their wellness goals. This doesn't even necessarily mean that you have to come up with your own product or service, in fact, companies such as Organo Gold have taken the hard work out of the process and done it for you. By discovering and researching very promising natural ingredients and figuring out how to incorporate them into already popular products, they've figured out how to make even better the products that millions of people already use every day.

Chapter 3 Behind the Curtain: The Organo Gold Team

The Organo Gold company was founded in 2008 by a network marketing industry (if you're unsure what that is, see upcoming chapter on the industry) veteran named Bernardo Chua. Chua was inspired by the book Think and Grow Rich, by Napoleon Hill. He's not the only one inspired by Hill, either. There are more than a million millionaires in the United States and many of them credit the book with turning things around for them in business.

Organo Gold was formed with the same goals in mind. As such, the company has formed a unique, unprecedented and exclusive collaboration with the Napoleon Hill Foundation. The Organo Gold founders believe in the 13 principles contained in the book to be essential in achieving personal and financial success. In addition, their principles are essential to accomplishing Organo Gold's mission of "Bringing the Treasures of the Earth to the People of the World."

The main treasure that Chua and Organo Gold want to share with the world is the wonders of the Ganoderma mushroom. Organo Gold is on a mission, to spread the knowledge of Ganoderma to the entire world. Using an effective network distribution system to deliver these products, more of every dollar the company makes is shared with their growing worldwide family.

Organo Gold is really like a global family and that family is growing every day. It's comprised of people who are caring and compassionate and believe that the knowledge of Ganoderma should be in the hands of people across the world, not just those who have had the privilege of stumbling on it themselves. It's a family that cares about each member and actually makes you feel a part of it.

CEO Bernardo "Bernie" Chua believes in working one person at a time, from the ground to the cup. He's a visionary who can often see things before the masses and knows when he comes across something that could change the future of the world. He feels he found such a thing with Ganoderma and considers it his duty to spread the benefits to as many people as he can reach. So far it's working, as he's been credited with introducing the concept of "Healthier Coffee" and "Ganoderma" to North America and the world on a mass scale.

I began drinking Organo Gold Healthy coffee in mid-June of 2009. My husband and I were introduced to the product through our oldest daughter's teacher. Her husband also ran fitness classes that I participated in. They are wonderful people!!! The very first drink I tried was the green tea. I enjoyed the taste and smoothness of the product. After finishing the cup I felt my body detox immediately. I needed water now! 1 hour after having drank the green tea I noticed that my muscles weren't nearly as tight and acidic feeling. I wish I could explain that better in words but I cannot. 4 hours later, the acidity returned. My husband, children and I left our 1st Healthy coffee party with a box of Black, Green Tea, Latte and Hot chocolate. We also left wanting to learn more about the business. My husband and I launched our own Organo Gold Healthy Coffee business on August 16, 2009. It has been going very well for us so far. Currently I drink 1-3 cups of Organo Gold every day. I have increased energy levels and stamina, two of the major benefits of consuming Ganoderma. I can feel my body regularly detoxifying - no tight acidic muscle feelings anymore and I crave water, lots of water! That's my Healthy Coffee story.

Corina W, Regina

In addition to being a visionary, a pioneer, and a leader, Bernie is a legend in the Direct Sales Industry, having proven himself by building a 500,000 Member Direct Sales Organization in the Philippines. He's been awarded the "Direct Sales Company of the Year" award for The Pacific Rim and Asia 5 times out of more than 1,600 companies. Additionally, he's often sought after for his decades of experience as a CEO and is exactly the type person you'd like at the helm of your company.

Due to his connectedness in the business world, he was able to found Organo Gold with an exclusive strategic alliance agreement with one of the largest certified Organic Ganoderma producers in the world. Having realized the benefits of it himself, he is dedicated to maximizing the potential of Ganoderma with research, development and an ever expanding line of scientifically developed Ganoderma based products that the public demands.

Under Bernie's innovative and dynamic leadership, Organo Gold is poised for unprecedented growth, unprecedented wealth creation with an unrivalled opportunity. Like any smart business person, however, Chua knows he can't go it alone. At least not with the global vision he has for the company. Joining Chua at the reins is co-founder Shane Morand. Those who have had the pleasure of getting to know Morand personally or professionally refer to him as a leader, recruiter, and mentor. Shane is a familiar face to just about everyone in the Organo Gold family.

At the young age of 25, Morand became the Vice President of Sales and Marketing for a major printing firm in Ottawa, Canada. There he assisted with and helped streamline the launching of the world's first and only North American television network dedicated to success. Having seen it first hand through his interactions with some of the industry's most high profile speakers and trainers including Anthony Robbins, Zig Ziglar, Mark Victor Hansen, Brian Tracy, Les Brown, Jim Rohn and Paul J. Myer, he understands goal achieving and success. He helped co-found Organo Gold in 2004 and has been enthusiastically introducing Healthier Coffee to North America as the company's Global Master Distributor ever since.

Vice President of Sales, Holton Buggs, is an experienced multi-level marketing executive with nearly two decades of experience. His dynamic innovation and strategic intelligence set him apart from his peers. To Organo Gold he brings a solid foundation of network marketing experience, having worked for 7 years with Amway.

Utilizing his specialized knowledge and passion, he's created Sales Team Systems that skyrocketed one company from sales of 6 million dollars to more than 50 million dollars. Holton has also built and mentored teams in excess of 100,000 with sales exceeding an enormous $100,000,000. He's published numerous books to give back to the industry and specializes in Leadership Development.

In addition to these three, Organo Gold works with a Scientific Advisory Board headed by chief medical consultant, Dr. Li Xiaoyu. The doctor oversees the center and certifies that the ingredients they use in their products are organic. In addition, Organo Gold works closely with a partner company in China founded by Li Ye and based out of the Xianzhilou Biology Research Center.

Thanks to the innovative and dynamic leadership of these men, Organo Gold is poised for unprecedented growth and wealth creation with an unrivalled opportunity. As such, it poses the question of whether you want to get involved and get your piece of the success. Think about your future. Where will you and your family be in 5 years from now? You may have a very clear vision of where you want to be but do you know how to get there? It's up to you to define your future, but Organo Gold can help turn that vision into a reality thanks to the wonders of the Ganoderma mushroom and their line of popular products.

I was introduced to Organo Gold from my sponsor, Theresa H. I can tell you I was very skeptical. I am someone that would have never tried this product on my own. I decided to try it based on Theresa, and drank it every day for a week. I seemed to have more energy every day and definitely would say that something

*was happening to my body. Just an overall feeling of "well-being".
I was sold. Now I have a Latte in the morning and drink the Green
Tea throughout the day. Thank you Organo Gold, Feeling Good!
Looking Good!*

Nancy R. Winnipeg, Canada

Chapter 4 The Ganoderma Mushroom

To fully understand the power of the Organo Gold product line, you must first understand the benefits of organically grown Ganoderma Lucidum. This mushroom is known by the Chinese as the "Miraculous King of Herbs" and it has stood the test of time, even among stiff competition with other Chinese wonder herbs. It's also known as lingzhi and is a large, bitter medicinal mushroom with shiny exterior.

Ganoderma Lucidum, photo taken by Eric Steinert

It's been used in Asia for more than 2000 and what the Chinese and Japanese have known for thousands of years has been backed up in modern clinical trial research studies that have shown it to be a cure-all kind of herb. While it cannot make you ageless or immortal, it has been referred to as a virtual elixir of life, it can save him from many fates worse than death such as AIDS, cancer and other fatal diseases. Unlike other options available today, it is safe to use for a long time and has no side effects in the recommended dose. This is quite preferable to modern drugs that oven have side effects more harmful or dangerous than the original ailment.

Instead of adverse side effects, the mushroom brings extra benefits such as energy restoration and increased stamina. It's due to these restorative properties that it's been combined with coffee, something else that brings health benefits.

While Ganoderma was discovered thousands of years ago, it was not available for common man due to its rarity. Since the mushroom grows on decaying wood in the dark and dense mountainous woods of high humidity in tropical and temperate regions of the world and takes nearly one year to mature, it could not preserve its nutrients from the surrounding environment and winds for a long time. In fact, the winds scattered its spores all around and these were often collected randomly along with foreign matter. Once the benefits were realized, Chinese herbalists had to trawl through lands to get the right mature wild Ganoderma to be served to Chinese emperors and royal officials.

I have never been a coffee drinker and not even a hot drink drinker. I had never heard of Ganoderma and had no idea what is was, did or was even about! Where am I getting this energy? Why am I still up when I have to get up so early? These were the questions I have been asking myself since taking Organo

Gold drinks. When I first started drinking the Green Tea and Mocha I found myself staying up later and later just getting more things done! I have to get up very early in the morning between 4:30 and 5:00 am. Even though when I would first wake up I knew I was tired I was able to get going and motivated right after I got up. Well after a few months I got lazy and wasn't making my tea and not drinking the Mocha as often and I couldn't figure out why I was getting so tired all of the time! It finally hit me, I wasn't drinking my Organo Gold! By the way, the iced green tea is wonderful but the Mocha is my favorite.

Vicki C, Lakewood, CO

It took years of rigorous research work on its cultured cultivation, but now Ganoderma is being grown indoors where high humidity and darkness are created for its better growth on a very large scale to meet its high pharmaceutical demand in the international medicine market. Special nets are used to cover the Ganoderma cultivation area to protect the spores from being scattered by winds. Now this 'plant of longevity or immortality' is within the easy access of common man at the health food stores and a few clicks away on Internet, such as through Organo Gold's product line. It's being produced not only in its native East Asian countries such as China, Japan, Korea, Taiwan and Malaysia but also in the U.S.

As for its benefits, these are numerous and impressive. Ganoderma may possess anti-tumor, immunomodulatory and immunotherapeutic activities, claims which are supported by studies on polysaccharides, terpenes, and other bioactive

compounds isolated from fruiting bodies and mycelia of this fun-
gus. It has also been found to inhibit platelet aggregation, and to
lower blood pressure, cholesterol, and blood sugar.

In addition, lab studies have shown anti-neoplastic effects against
some types of cancer, possibly preventing metastasis, though the
mechanisms are unknown and may target different stages of cancer development, whether it be through inhibiting the formation of
new, tumor-induced blood vessels created to supply nutrients to
the tumor, inhibiting migration of the cancer cells or inducing and
enhancing apoptosis of tumor cells. Regardless of how
Ganoderma works, it's currently being used in commercial phar-
maceuticals for suppressing cancer cell proliferation and migration.

Though impressive, the benefits of this 'supernatural mushroom'
don't end here. Other studies indicate that it may protect against
liver injury by viruses and other toxic agents, suggesting a potential benefit of this compound in the treatment of liver disease. It's
also reported to have anti-bacterial and anti-viral activities, exhib-
iting direct anti-viral effects to HSV and influenza viruses, to name
a few. Ganoderma is also believed to lower high blood pressure,
cholesterol, and have anti-inflammatory benefits.

In a nutshell, Ganoderma has the following health benefits:

- Promotes normal immune function
- Supports stamina and endurance
- Supports memory and focus
- Promotes a healthy digestive system
- Helps support and protect liver function
- Is rich in fiber, minerals, and other nutrients

Due to the bitter taste of this 'magic mushroom,' Ganoderma is usually prepared as a hot water extract product, adding a thinly sliced or pulverized mushroom (either fresh or dried) to a pot of boiling water, which is then allowed to simmer for several hours, sometimes repeated for additional concentration. It's also often used to make an extract in liquid, capsule, or powder form. These are the ways that Ganoderma is incorporated into Organo Gold's exclusive line of products.

Because of my job I am going in and out of places all day long. The challenge for me from my job is that my body has to adjust very quickly to different temperatures. Last week I was exposed to a lot of rain throughout the day. As a result by the time I arrived home I was feeling very sick. I went to sleep immediately. After a few minutes I was completely congested. I was not able to breathe. I panicked. As I child I had asthma and I felt how difficult it was becoming for me to breathe. My daughters made me a cup of mocha and 2 Ganoderma capsules. Within 15 minutes I started to feel better and able to breathe. Within 20 to 30 minutes I was completely clear and able to breathe normally. Those who have never had asthma have no idea how scary it is to experience the feeling of not being able to breathe. I am very grateful to have Organo Gold in my life.

Gabby R, Illinois

Chapter 5 Organo Gold's Products

Each product in Organo Gold's line is unique and appealing to large amounts of people. We'll address each product separately as it helps get a feel for the company overall and the types of products that are sold by the network marketing company. The products can be broken into three separate categories, these being Beverages, Nutraceuticals, and Personal Care products. Each of these categories appeals to some of the same people and some unique people, which makes Organo Gold's demographic wide ranging. Discussion of why these types of products have been chosen will follow in a separate chapter but first we'll look at each product individually.

Organo Gold's beverage category is known as "where Ancient China meets modern science." Heading up this category is Gourmet Café Supreme, which features the Superior Panax Ginseng plant. This has long been considered an herb of great value and in the ancient world it was only available to people of great power and privilege. It's still highly prized and treasured in Asia as a source of health and well-being. By combining this powerful herb with Organo Gold's exclusive certified, authentic, and organic Ganoderma, the result is a smooth latte blend that is perfect for coffee drinkers looking for a natural lift to their day.

The next option in the beverage line is plain Black Coffee which awakens the senses. It has a dark smooth taste and deep aroma that is infused Ganoderma, introducing coffee lovers to a new and delicious alternative. With OG's Black Coffee, you can enjoy the taste of freshly brewed coffee, but do so instantly.

You know that I am the number one fan of Ganoderma, since I have been taking it - I am unstoppable!!   I have never had so much energy, I am healthy, my hair looks great, my nails grow fast and strong. People think that I am 24 not the 42. I am a 'gym bunny' 7 days a week, I have started to run almost 30km per week, sometimes more. I have never felt better in my life, I want everyone I know to feel this energy and feel this good every day!!

Anne B, Nanaimo

One of the most popular options is the Gourmet Café Mocha, which is known as "Dessert in a Cup". This aromatic coffee is combined with the finest cocoa to bring about a guilt-free mocha. Combining a sweet, rich coffee taste with authentic Ganoderma makes for the perfect energizing after-dinner drink.

Another delicious option is the Gourmet Latte. This one is a favorite of Organo Gold employees and it blends high quality aromatic Arabica coffee beans with authentic Ganoderma. It's perfect for breakfast or as a relaxing drink, as the coffee is light, sweet, and creamy making it the ideal start for any morning.

For all the chocolate lovers out there, Organo Gold has just the thing for you: Gourmet Hot Chocolate. This delicious drink offers a unique blend of smooth, rich chocolatey taste and authentic Ganoderma. It'll warm your body during cold days and is a great tasting drink that everyone can enjoy. In fact, a chocolate based drink was so highly requested that the company decided to create one to suit those desires.

For those who aren't partial to coffee or chocolate, Organo Gold offers plenty of tea options, such as their Organic Red Tea. This product combines organic red tea leaves with Ganoderma and another incredible ingredient called Cordyceps militaris, which has an equally well-respected history in China. The combination of these two special ingredients is the perfect tea to maintain balance and clarity in the body.

Green tea is one of the most mainstream types of tea and it should be expected that Organo Gold would have an offering. Their Organic Green Tea is exceptionally soothing and full of flavor, with the added benefit of including Organic Ganoderma to a beverage already rich with anti-oxidants.

But the Organo Gold beverage product line doesn't stop there. Next up is the King of Coffee, which is exclusively produced by the company. It features Premium Organic Coffee infused with Certified Ganoderma Spore Powder and offers a lighter coffee taste and fresh aroma, making it fantastic paired with any food.

No line of coffee drinks would be complete without an Arabica bean offering. Organo Gold's Premium Gourmet Royal Brewed option takes advantage of the fact that Jamaica has been perfecting their coffee bean farming for over 100 years. In order to ensure premium quality, workers individually hand sort the rich Arabica beans before the coffee is processed with some of the most rigorous quality standards in the world. The result is a fresh taste and rich aroma that is second to none. By infusing Jamaica Blue Mountain® Coffee with authentic Ganoderma Spore Powder and using only the highest quality ingredients available, Organo Gold's Premium Gourmet Royal Brewed Coffee is a brew fit for royalty.

Making sure to cover all the bases, Black Ice is the perfect beverage for a hot summer day. It provides a cool blast of refreshing black tea, but contains no artificial sweeteners, just pure, natural honey. Adding in Ganoderma and Amazonian guarana, Black Ice will make you want to seize the day and conquer anything that comes your way.

#1 Energy Boost

I'm a nurse and my normal routine is to work three 12-hour shifts on the weekends. Usually I get one good night's sleep on Thursday night. Then I go go go all weekend, working Fri, Sat & Sun nights with activities planned in between. I allow my body very little rest and have been known to spend the Monday after the last shift nearly exhausted, and "crashing" by Monday evening.

Since enjoying the Organo Gold coffee and tea, I have noticed that I have more energy during my "marathon" weekends. I don't feel tired on Monday, even after working all weekend.

#2 Efficient Bowels

Again, being a nurse and I tend to notice things some would dismiss, like how my body is eliminating waste. Since consuming the

Organo Gold beverages, I have noticed my bowels moving more often, with more output and less effort. I know, like I said before, not a subject most want to talk about. But everyone does it, ideally at least daily, if not more than once a day.

Collette G, California

As you can see, Organo Gold covers the beverage category quite comprehensively, but the company doesn't stop there. A variety of nutraceutical options are also available and will be discussed next.

Grape seed Oil has been acclaimed for millennia as being an incredibly versatile natural oil. As expected it comes from the seeds of grapes and is naturally rich in phytochemicals and polyunsaturated fatty acids, in addition to containing many of the important building blocks of life. Taking one of these capsules daily will ensure a person is getting all of these essential nutrients.

Next up is Ganoderma Lucidum Mycelium, which is a pill taken from an 18-day old Ganoderma Lucidum mushroom with a naturally high concentration of Germanium and Polysaccharides such as beta-glucan.

It's also possible to purchase the Ganoderma Sport Powder, which you may remember from some of the products in the beverage line. It's derived from the seeds of the Ganoderma Lucidum mushroom and cultivated from natural log wood. It's then extracted through low-temperature, shell-broken technology, allowing the extract to reach as high as 99.9% purity. It's Certified Organic by China, U.S., Japan, and the E.U. and is naturally rich in Ganoderma Lucidum Polysaccharides, Triterpenes, Germanium and Selenium.

Rounding out the nutraceutical category is straight Ganoderma Lucidum, which is most potent health booster and overall conditioner. It's often associated with longevity, youthfulness, and vitality and has been revered for over 5,000 years as the highest ranking "Superior Herb" in the ancient books of herbs and medicine.

Finally, as discussed earlier, millions of people are in the market for personal beauty and care products and the benefits of Ganoderma even extend to these arenas. The first product to note is OG Smile, which is a toothpaste with authentic Ganoderma and the fresh taste of mint developed for the special care of teeth and gums. In addition to the aforementioned, it contains natural products that promote oral health and leave the user with whiter teeth and fresher breath.

Next up is G3 Premium Beauty Soap that uses a unique combination of Glutathione, Grapeseed, and Ganoderma Lucidum Extract to cleanse, moisturize, and promote skin's youthful vibrancy. It's also hypoallergenic.

Lastly is Velvet, a body lotion that leaves skin feeling smooth and soft all over. As mentioned in an earlier chapter, skin care is of the utmost importance to millions of people, especially the female Baby Boomer population who is concerned about having youthful looking skin. The Ganoderma in this lotion nourishes skin cells while macadamia nut oil gives it a moisture-rich boost. Lastly, collagen is used to increase elasticity to help with the quest for the eternally youthful look.

As you can see, the Organo Gold product lines are very comprehensive and including something for everyone (and more than one thing for most people). Regardless of age, sex, location, or goals, there's an Organo Gold product featuring Ganoderma that can benefit anyone.

I have osteo-arthritis/porosis, fibromyalgia, and degenerative disc disease in my upper and lower back as well as bilateral carpal tunnel syndrome. Due to the pain, I had to quit my Assistant Manager's Position in Dec. 06 because I could no longer stand the long hours. Nor could I count the money or hold the boxes I needed to in order to pack in the customers' orders. By the time my short term disability ran out I was still unable to return to work and we have been struggling on one income ever since. Because of the major pain and the medications I was taking I was spending more time in bed than out of it. I could not empty the dishwasher without having to sit down in between because it hurt my back so much. Vacuuming took me forever as I had to stop and sit several times to rest my back. The usual household chores that we normally take for granted were very painful for me.

I was introduced to Organo Gold in April. I started with one cup of coffee which gave me energy right away.

I did not expect to sleep that night because anytime I drink coffee or tea after 1 in the afternoon I am awake all night long. Well, let me tell you, I slept like a baby. I could not believe it. However, as usual come morning I awoke with my normal pains and numbness in my legs and arms. I asked my husband to bring me a cup of Organo Gold Gourmet Black Coffee before he left for work and before I was half way through the cup I was up out of bed before I even realized it. I couldn't believe it! Half a cup of coffee got me up before 8 AM. Normally I was in bed till 10 or 11 am. Now, I am drinking the coffee all day and taking one of each capsule. I take my Gourmet Black coffee sachets with me everywhere I go.

I went outside one day at 9:30 am planning to do some weeding for a couple of hours before it got too hot. By the time I couldn't stand it anymore, my legs were so sore from stretching, kneeling, and bending and my hands could not pull one more weed, I could barely make it back into the house. You know what? I looked at the clock expected it to be about 11:30-12:00? It was almost 2pm! I was outside for 4 1/2 hours! Never in my life have I spent that much time weeding, not ever. Not even as a child. By the way, I was diagnosed with arthritis in my feet at the age of twelve.

It's been like that for me all summer, I'm either weeding, or painting the walls/trim inside the house, or housework, baking. I can't sit still. I'm hardly ever at the computer, I used to be sitting in front of the computer or in bed most of the day.

That's not all, my husband Ray is 65.   His blood pressure has dropped 20 points and he swears his hair is growing back on his head, his arms and shoulders are growing "peach fuzz" and he also has more energy without the jitters that regular coffee gives a person. Ray's doctor was monitoring his prostate "PSA" levels without us knowing about it. He was sending him for what we thought were routine blood tests for cholesterol. His PSA levels we found out after the third one were 4.2, 6.4, 10.4. After the third one the doctor was very concerned at the possibility of prostate cancer. He wanted Ray to go for one more blood test "when he found the time". I doubled up his intake of spores and Ganoderma capsules and told him to drink more coffee during the day. A few weeks later he went for his blood tests. We didn't hear from the doctor after a couple weeks so Ray phoned and the receptionist told him that the tests were normal. He didn't get that dreaded phone call - "can you come in? The Doctor would like to speak to you".

That was a couple of months ago. Ray continues to take two spores, two Ganoderma, one grapeseed oil extract and one myselium capsule daily. I take one of each and we both drink coffee all day. Primarily black, Ray likes latte too and I mix and match depending on my mood.

Sandra P, Wembley

It'd undeniable that the Organo Gold products are delicious but it may seem curious as to why they've chosen to combine the power of the Ganoderma mushroom with beverages like coffee and tea. However, if you think about it, you'll probably be hard-pressed to think of anyone you know who doesn't like coffee, tea, hot chocolate, or all of the above. As such, this beverage line is actually an ingenious way to spread the wonders of Ganoderma to all the world.

Looking at the statistics, it's even more convincing that this line of products is the best way to go. Coffee is one of the world's most consumed beverages after water and is the world's largest traded commodity after oil, beating out commodities like natural gas, gold, brent oil, sugar and corn.

In North America alone, nearly half a billion cups, or close to 3 billion pounds, are consumed by more than 80% of people over the age of 18 each year, meaning there are 255 million coffee drinkers on the continent. The U.S. is the largest coffee consumer, valued at about $19 billion each year, buying about one-fifth of the world's annual coffee crop which takes up more than 25 million acres across more than 90 nations. Many of these people are already willing to shell out $4 per cup and American coffee drinkers average 3 and a half cups every day, with some spending up to $20 in a single day on coffee. In addition, specialty coffee sales are increasing by 20% per year, which means people are interested in fancier options and are willing to pay more for them. In fact, gourmet coffees account for about half of that industry value. Food enthusiasts are trying to increase that value even more by promoting new coffee-industry trends such as pairing specific coffee blends with food, or as with Organo Gold, combining coffee with the healthy Ganderma mushroom.

Since I have been drinking Organo Gold coffee I feel a lot better less stress and lower blood pressure. I have been using the product for about 6 weeks and have found a significant change with in me. I have also lost approx. 8 pounds and still losing weight - it feels great.

Bob P, Magnolia, Texas

Coffee shops have popped up on just about every street corner in recent years which is as great indicator of how the coffee industry is booming. They're actually the fastest growing niche in the restaurant business and have a seven percent annual growth rate. In addition, other establishments are trying to get into the coffee game, as well. You'll notice that convenience store chains often have entire sections devoted to a variety of coffee options, as well as a variety of flavors and sizes. Fast food restaurants, too, are trying not to miss out on the millions of dollars that consumers are willing to spend on the drinks and are offering full coffee lines with lattes and mochas and more. And with Americans consuming 400 million cups of coffee daily, which equals about four-and-a-half thousand cups of coffee each second, you can see why.

You'd be hard pressed to be back to get from work to your house without encountering a handful of places to get a cup of coffee. Even if you work at home, you likely have a coffee maker or at the very least, instant coffee in your cupboard.

Interestingly, coffee came to America with the tastes of the British. In the middle 1700s, tea and coffee were equally favored and many taverns doubled as coffee houses. As a result of the famous Boston Tea Party, however, when a large shipment of tea was dumped into Boston harbor to protest the British tax on tea, proclaiming "no taxation without representation", it became unpatriotic to drink tea. Colonists soon found that they could import coffee grown in Central and South America and by the beginning of the 1900s, America was consuming 1/2 of all coffee produced in the world.

Prior to that point, however, drinking tea had been just as popular in the United States as it was in England. The history of tea is actually long and complex, spreading across many cultures and spanning thousands of years. Similar to Ganoderma, tea originated in China as a medicinal drink, with the earliest credible records dating back to the 3rd century AD. When drinking tea became popular in Britain during the 17th century, they're the ones who introduced tea to India in an effort to compete with the Chinese monopoly on it. As mentioned, the British originally brought tea with them to the US and while in present day, coffee is much more popular, teas are still enjoyed both with meals and as refreshments.

In fact, although the popularity of coffee is very hard to rival, tea has some pretty impressive statistics, as well. 519 million pounds of tea are imported to the U.S. each year for total sales of $15 billion annually. 3,000 million tons of tea is produced each year worldwide by the 2 billion morning tea drinkers. An impressive 1.42 million pounds of tea are consumed in the U.S. each day.

There are also a lot of interesting and intriguing things to know about hot chocolate, and chocolate in general. The average American eats 10-12 pounds and is the food most commonly craved by women (who, you might remember, are the demographic most frequently researching the wellness industry and willing to spend the most on wellness products).

We love the taste on Organo Gold coffee!! We have more energy, we sleep better than ever before and wake up refreshed.

Regarding our kids, I gave my 10 year old the mycelium for focus in school, after 3 days she started requesting the "vitamin" because she didn't have headaches during the day when she took them I didn't even know she was having headaches at school.

Miles and Jackie A, Magnolia, Texas

Chocolate actually has some health benefits of its own, having been shown in several medical studies to prolong life by reducing risk of blood clots and fighting bad cholesterol. Very popular, as well, U.S. manufacturers use 3.5 million pounds of whole milk every day to make chocolate. Children are more likely to prefer chocolate when they reach 10-11 years old than when they are younger, so Organo Gold's hot chocolate option can be a great way to encourage children to get the health benefits of Ganoderma without introducing them to coffee or tea at a young age. Chocolate is America's favorite flavor, according to recent surveys with a little over 50% of adults preferring chocolate to other flavors.

As you can see, it's no accident that the Organo Gold line of products is based on coffee, tea, and hot chocolate. These make up multi-billion dollar industries and just about everyone in the developed world enjoys one of these three beverages, if not two or all three of them. As such, it makes selling the products a breeze, since it's something you customers would be spending money on already, so it's not an additional expense, it's actually just utilizing the money elsewhere to buy a better version of the same thing.

Chapter 7 Why Selling Organo Products is so Easy

Speaking of selling, Organo Gold actually makes it very easy to encourage people to buy your products, as they promote sampling. This means you're actually giving away packets of the coffee and other products to perspective customers so that they can, in essence, try before they buy.

Sales is an interesting industry, and many people think they need to be a "salesperson" in order to be successful. This is untrue. When you're selling a product that you believe in and know it can help people, it becomes easy to strike up a conversation about how it can help your future customer. The benefits of the Ganoderma mushroom can help improve millions of lives and it should be considered a great opportunity to be able to share the benefits with as many people as possible. Conversations shouldn't be approached as sales pitches, but as chances to show a new person the wonders of the Organo Gold product line.

In addition, when it does come time to ask whether the person is interested in making a purchase, it can help a great deal to understand the science behind sales and what, exactly, makes a person buy something. Much like any other skill, sales can be learned and practiced until it becomes second nature.

I started drinking coffee with Ganoderma Organo Gold in 2008 because it was healthier. Little did I know at the time what a benefit it was to my body. My seasonal allergies were almost nonexistent but at the time I didn't realize it was because of the Ganoderma. The following year I took a hiatus from drinking the coffee and my allergies were back full force. Shortly after that I went to an Organo Gold event and learned the why and how behind Ganoderma. I immediately went back to drinking my one cup of Organo Gold coffee a day, and I started to pay attention to how my body was feeling.

Here's a list of changes that I've noticed:

• No coffee jitters!!

• My seasonal allergies are controlled.

• I have noticed that I no longer need a lunch or after work coffee to help me keep going.

• I no longer need a 'cat nap' after work.

• My heart is working less hard – my heart rate at work is now in the low 70's versus the low 90's when I was drinking regular coffee.

• It is easy for me to jump on the elliptical machine and hammer out a 25 minute cardio workout even though I'm guilty of owning a gym membership that I hardly use.

• I lost about 5 pounds without changing my habits.

• I use much less lotion and lip balm since I am now better hydrated with Organo Gold versus regular coffee.

• Lastly, my mood is improved and I feel better overall.

I am now starting to take the capsules once a day and can't believe the energy I have! I work in the front lines of an acute care hospital and I truly believe that the immune boosting benefits will help me stay healthy and able to combat whatever Mother Nature throws my way! So far I haven't been sick since I restarted Organo Gold and I'm looking forward to keeping it that way!

Nadeane N, Regina

People buy products that fulfill their basic needs. While these initially meant food and shelter, the dependence that most people have on caffeine, in general, and coffee, specifically, make it a necessity for millions. People also buy based on convenience. While there are coffee shops on every corner, nothing is more convenient than a product you can make at home or take with you to make on the job or vacation. Rather than going out of one's way or spending time waiting in line for a coffee, people will spend money to get it as easily and quickly as possible. In addition, people are willing to spend a little more for the convenience.

People buy to replace things that they've had and either need to replace or just get more of. Coffee is one such thing. Most people have likely purchased coffee products for their home in the past, but may be running low or out completely and need more. This is an aspect that you can play up during the sales process, as maybe they've taken to spending more money or time to get coffee since they've run out of the kind they can make at home. Organo Gold products can solve this problem.

Another reason people buy things is because they are valuable or rare. Organo Gold products are both of these things. A price cannot even be put on the health benefits of Ganoderma and the way it will improve one's life. In addition, Organo Gold is the only company that distributes Ganoderma in coffee products, making it relatively scarce. Potential customers will know that they can't say no to you and go to the local grocery store and buy it themselves, they'll need to take advantage of the opportunity to purchase it while they can.

I have had some medical issues since 1987 and this coffee has actually taken away my dizziness and hot flashes!! I do have more energy in the day...no doubt about it. I don't care how much it costs...I will not go without it. I had my parents try it and they drink it every day and have noticed more energy!! I wish everyone would try this coffee and products...it really could change your life!

Heather K, Calgary

As I researched Organo Gold, I met with a number of people selling the product. Each of whom I asked how did they sell/retail their products? Nearly all of them had the same answer. I thought I would offer you one example, just to show how simple the process is. This was a lady named Sally, from Reno, and I'll share with you our conversation.

Most people don't like selling to their friends and family, yet lots of people seem to join up ORGANO GOLD because of their friends and family, why is this Sally?

Coffee is a universal product, everybody knows about coffee, tea or hot chocolate. There is no difficult explanation required. It's easy, simple, its…coffee.

While it true, most of us don't like 'selling', nor do we want to appear like a pushy sales person… most of us dislike sales because of 'fear of rejection' and or being judged. We don't want to be seen as having 'dollar signs in our eyes' or our friends or family will run from us, and rightly so. It's not something I want to see from a friend myself.

So, I don't sell. I inform. I make sure I let my warm market family, friends, associates and referrals know that I am in the 'coffee business' and I want them to try my coffee, and if they like it, to buy my coffee. It's no different from if I owned a coffee shop.

Now, something that helps me here is my belief in my products. It's solid. I love our coffee, and I love what it does for people. I am a really a product of the product. Sure, there are a lot of different coffees in the market place - but what makes my coffee so unique is the ingredients in the coffee and how proven healthy it is. So I am able to offer a product that address two major areas:

1. The love people have for coffee - every day and 2. At the same time helping sustain or improve their health without trying to alter their lives. People are addicted to coffee. So why not just drink mine? My attitude is that everyone should be drinking it. The evidence is striking.

I tell Sally that that makes sense, but, I ask, 'how do you bring up your coffee? Take me through a way you might get someone to try it? In other words, what do you say to start a conversation to someone to get that person to try your coffee?'

'Easy, she says. 'I ask 4 simple questions:'

1. Do you or any you know drink coffee or tea at least occasionally?

2. How do you drink your coffee? (i.e. black, or with cream and sugar?

3. What's your favorite brand?

4. When was the last time (name of their brand) sent you a check for drinking or recommending their coffee?

Ok, that sounds easy, and that would provoke a smile, what comes next, I asked her.

"Easy again, I show them the 'sample' and say: "This is the coffee that Pays You"

Now, before giving them a sample, I say: "I would like to give you a sample and I will follow up after you drink the coffee to get two pieces of information from you:

How did you like the taste?

How did it make you feel?

People love free samples, and are usually very happy to get free coffee, especially now that it is so expansive. So now I just ask:

"What is the best time to call you so you can tell me how you liked it?

In the morning or afternoon?"

Then I make sure I follow up."

In addition, many people will have already heard of Organo Gold products by the time you approach them about sampling the product and making a purchase. As such, you'll have the benefit of name recognition. With well-connected people heading the company and producing a product unrivaled in the consumer world, it's likely that the company's reputation will have preceded you. That makes for an easy sale, as the person will not need to be told of the benefits of Ganoderma, but instead will already know them and be eager to try the product. In addition, as this is still a relatively exclusive product, some people may be interested in buying it in order to impress their friends or have something new and innovative that others don't. Many people who are very into high end coffee are always looking for the next big thing and will want to be the person who brings word of Organo Gold to all their coffee drinking friends, rather than hearing about it from someone else. It can help people bond over a common interest, such as coffee drinking, and on the flip side of that, some people may want to buy the product because all of their friends have and they don't want to be left out.

Whether someone is interested in buying the product because they're addicted to caffeine and need the coffee or whether they're just in the mood for a little bit of luxury and want to indulge in a high quality product that will improve their health, there is no shortage of reasons that people buy things. By learning how to read the customer, you'll know what approach to take. If someone really loves coffee, it's easy to talk about how delicious the product tastes and then offer a sample to back it up. If someone is really into doing things that are good for their health, they'll love to hear about the benefits of Ganoderma. If someone likes to be a trendsetter, it'll help to hear about how innovative this product is and how they'd be the first one to introduce it to all of their friends.

When I first heard about healthy coffee my first reaction was that I don't even drink coffee and how in the world can COFFEE be HEALTHY!!! However, I WAS a big Energy Drink fan Monster, Red Bull, etc., so when I was told that this coffee would give me energy I gave it a shot. I drank it and had a TON of Energy almost the entire day and never got jitters, shakes, or crash like I normally did drinking my energy drinks. Then a few days later I realized that I had also not been hitting snooze and falling back off in the morning. I would be up for good as soon as my alarm would go off. Darn Ganoderma!! Now, I cannot start my day without a hot cup of Organo Gold and my Organo Gold capsules!

Brett S, Richmond, Texas

By allowing for and encouraging sampling, Organo Gold shows that it's confident in its product line and isn't worried that people will be disappointed by the taste. A lesser company would make a strong sales pitch but then not allow the potential customer to try the product before buying it, at which point it would be too late if the person was displeased. Organo Gold is different because their products are solid. Instead of having to hide behind packaging and fluff, founders of the company are eager to have people try their products because at that point, they'll sell themselves. People will love the delicious aromas and tastes of the products, as well as the variety of options available. There's something for everyone and every different taste. The sampling will convince people that just because Ganoderma is so great for their health, doesn't mean it's going to ruin a drink that they would otherwise enjoy. In fact, they'll likely get even more enjoyment out of knowing how good it is for their health. Sampling takes a lot of the pressure off the salesperson and puts it on the quality of the product. When you sell a product that meets and exceeds all of the claims that it makes, sales are a breeze.

I wasn't a coffee drinker prior to April 19, 2009 when I was introduced to the healthy coffee of Organo Gold. I was diagnosed with an enlarged prostate almost 20 years ago, I recently had my follow-up appointment from January 2009; on Tuesday June 23, 2009. I was examined by my doctor and was told my prostate was normal. I was asked what I had been doing differently since the last visit, if anything. A lot of praying and drinking healthy coffee and gave him a sample of the Latte, because that's what I drink.

Ron C, Houston, Texas

Chapter 8 How products are moved to the Consumer via the Network Marketing Industry

Many people have never heard of networking marketing and other people have heard incorrect or negative things about the industry that dissuade people from becoming interested. Here we'll discuss what the network marketing industry actually is and why it is a good industry to be involved in. It's a widely accepted industry and millions of people are already making money through this legitimate type of business.

With network marketing, the sales force is compensated not only for sales they personally generate, but also for the sales of the other salespeople that they have recruited to the company. The recruited sales force is referred to as the participant's "downline", and can provide multiple levels of compensation. In essence, when you start selling the product, you can recruit other people to do so, as well, and when you do, you receive a percentage of their sales, as well, meaning you make money whenever they make sales, not just when you do.

Salespeople are expected to sell the products directly to consumers by means of relationship referrals and word of mouth, making network marketing a form of direct sales. Salespeople work independently and are not salaried. They are referred to as distributors, associates, independent business owners, dealers, franchise owners, or independent agents, etc. They represent the company (in this case, Organo Gold) that produces the products they sell. Distributors are awarded a commission based upon the volume of product sold through their own sales efforts as well as that of their downline organization.

Independent distributors develop their organizations by either building an active customer base of people who buy directly from the company and do so repeatedly and consistently, or by recruiting a "downline" of other distributors who also build a customer base, thereby expanding the overall organization. Additionally, since distributors purchase products at a wholesale price, they can also earn a profit selling these products at retail prices.

For the last 6 years or so, I have had the beginnings of gum disease. Since my dentist first told me, I have been flossing more often to make sure to keep the plaque and bacteria away from the gums. For all of this time, there has ALWAYS been slight bleeding when I floss and when I brush. Last month I noticed something. I was brushing my teeth one night when I looked down into the sink and realized that there was no blood. Then I thought about it, and realized that I didn't remember bleeding for quite a while...weeks and maybe even a few months. This hasn't happened in 6 years! Coincidentally, the only different habit I've had has been consuming Ganoderma through Organo Gold Coffee and the Capsules.

Dave D.

It should be clear at this point that network marketing is not a scam, as some negative publicity will have you believe. In fact, it's a great way to leverage your network of friends, family, coworkers, and other acquaintances into a profitable business by providing them with a product that they're already buying! In addition, you're allowing them to get in on the profits by joining the company themselves and becoming part of your "downline" team. Even Donald Trump understands the power and potential of network marketing; when he was asked recently what he would do if he had it to do all over again, his matter-of-fact, one-line answer was: "I would get into network marketing." That's a powerful sentiment coming from such a wealthy and successful business person.

In addition, Robert Kiyosaki has said, "Network promoting gives folk the possibility, with extraordinarily low risk and very low monetary obligation, to build their own income-generating asset and acquire great wealth." Why wouldn't you want to experience that kind of opportunity and potential yourself?

The power and potential of network marketing is even taught in college business classes as it's the wave of the future. It's the fastest growing financial model in the world today and the most vital of all entrepreneurial opportunities available today. That's not to say that it's easy, but to quote Donald Trump again, "I am frequently questioned if Social marketing is a Pyramid scheme. You're either a real expert in cash or enslaved by it. A firm has only one person at the top, generally the manager, and everybody else below." Why continue to be a part of a firm with just one person making the big bucks at the top when you could participate in network marketing and get as much of the profits as you decide to work for. Distributors even have the opportunity to start their businesses part-time at first and then potentially do if full-time if they so choose. Once distributors reach a point of relative success, they can help others start their part time businesses. This sure beats taking orders from someone else for the rest several decades.

After only a few days of drinking the Organo Gold coffee I can't believe how much more energy I have. I also seem to be able to concentrate a lot better. If this can happen after just a few days, I can only imagine the effects of Organo Gold coffee after a longer period of time."

Janis A, Ajax, Ontario

Harvard Business School did a study on network marketing and what factors to look for in a business before getting involved. Organo Gold checks out. One of the most successful indicators to make a network marketing company the most desirable is that the company must be at least 18 months old. As you'll remember from an earlier chapter, Organo Gold has been in business for nearly a decade, meaning it's stood the test of time and proven itself in the competitive world of network marketing. 90% of all network marketing companies fail in the first year and a half due to inadequate financing and inexperienced senior management. Thanks to decades of business and network marketing specific experience in the founders and senior management of Organo Gold, it's been able to not only stay afloat, but profit, flourish, and grow, leaving it poised for unprecedented growth, wealth creation, and unrivalled opportunity.

Another indicator of success for a network marketing company is having a product that is both unique and highly consumable. Hopefully you recognize by now that Organo Gold products are exactly those things. They are exclusive products purchased only from approved distributors with repeated sales, which guarantees customer loyalty. This is opposed to a one-time sale and having to locate and develop new customers over and over in order to be successful. With Organo Gold, once you locate your network, you'll make money each and every time they buy the product, or whenever someone buys the product through someone in your "downside" network. You won't have to go around reinventing the wheel for every sale; once potential customers are encouraged to sample the product the first time, they'll be hooked and become loyal customers forever more.

Lastly, you want to make sure that you have the opportunity to get in on the business on the ground floor. Obviously you want to devote your energies to an area that is not already saturated with distributors so that you can make more money. This means that the company should have less than 1.5 million distributors in order for it to be a worthy investment of your time, which Organo Gold is.

Hopefully by now you realize that network marketing is not the negative business model that you may have heard about. In fact, it is one of the fastest growing models of the past few decades, with revenues growing by 7.1% annually, which is dramatically above the rate of growth of the overall economy. Direct selling sales total more than $29 billion, or roughly 1% of total U.S. retail sales. In fact, more than 50% of American adults have purchased goods or services from a direct selling representative at some time. Clearly people are willing to participate in network marketing businesses, especially when the product is worthy, which Organo Gold's are.

I have been using Organo Gold products for just over a week Gourmet Black Coffee 2-3 cups daily and Mycelium 3 capsules twice daily. I was an avid coffee drinker 4-6 cups per day and have not had a cup of traditional coffee in over 10 days. I DID NOT EXPERIENCE ANY CAFFEINE WITHDRAWAL! Physically, I feel great with a significant increase in energy, an improved general sense of well-being, improved sleep and enhanced focus and mental clarity. Furthermore, previous to starting on the Organo Gold product I was on week 4 of significant allergy symptoms and a common cold. These symptoms completely disappeared within 2 days of being on the product just 2 cups of Organo Gold Gourmet Black Coffee per day at that point.

As a healthcare professional and educator, I was a bit curious with regards to the active ingredient in the product Ganoderma Lucidum so I did some research. Although I referenced many sources, I thought it fitting to cite one Herbs Explained by Martin Stone. From this source I quote a description, "It Ganoderma Lucidum has been popular for at least two thousand years in the Far East, and is considered the premier example of a superior herb. A superior herb is considered the highest classification...."

Kirk D, Okotoks

Chapter 9 How To Succeed At Network Marketing and Organo Gold

There are several ways that you can be an effective network marketer and learn from successful experts before you. One of the best ways to look at it is to recognize that every business is a relationship-based business. In fact, Robert Kiyosaki is quoted as saying, ""The wealthiest folks in the world look for and build networks, and everyone else looks for work." While obviously the product you're selling is important, so is developing functional relationships with your present and future clients. It's a known fact that people are more likely to buy from people whom they trust, so gaining this trust through relationship development is one of the biggest considerations in network marketing.

In addition, it's important to think analytically about your network. The most successful distributors penetrate untouched markets and then work hard to gain a high market share in whatever that market is. This will allow word of mouth in that network to spread more rapidly about the value of your product, whereby bringing in more business to you. Essentially, you're allowing your network to go to work and work for you, which is the basis of network marketing.

It's a great idea to create a community around your product, as this will increase awareness and bring potential clients to you. One way to do this would be to host coffee mixers at your home or office where you'll be able to introduce potential new clients to the products and their health benefits, encourage them to sample the products to see how delicious they are, and purchase them themselves. It also allows the opportunity to recruit new members to your "downline" team.

A little over a year ago I developed an abscess on my gum line. It looked almost like a large blister on my gum line. After having it for about 6 months I finally decided to go to the dentist, who said he hadn't ever seen anything like it. However, he wasn't sure if it was something that would require a root canal or if it was an issue with my gums, so he referred me to a specialist. I never went. To be truthful, life was too busy...the abscess didn't hurt....and I would have had to pay a somewhat significant out of pocket amount to go to the specialist. I figured I'd just "deal" until it started to hurt.

Fast forward several months...I started drinking the Organo Gold Black coffee on occasion. Then I started to take the Spores on a daily basis. Within a week of taking the Spores, my abscess seems to have disappeared. I had it for about 15 months without any signs of it going away...only to rub my tongue over it after a week on the Spores to find my gums were smooth. I suppose it could be a coincidence.

Dawn M, Thornton, CO

Additionally, network marketing provides great opportunities to demographics who are unlike the traditional American corporate sales force. Whereas corporate salespeople are generally male and have higher levels of education, 80% of direct selling sales forces are female and 56% do not have any higher education. The benefit here is that the customer demographic of network

marketing companies is just like the sales force, making distributors very effective salespeople, as they're able to sell to their own
communities. Common culture and interests create a foundation
to build strong relationships more quickly, and as discussed earlier, relationships are the foundation of a successful network marketing career. This is not to say that men with higher educations
are not, or should not, be involved with the industry, it just means
there are opportunities for people of all walks of life that may not
be available in other industries.

Another benefit of network marketing and simple way to be successful is to leverage personal relationships first. While a delicate
task, many people are more comfortable practicing their relationship building and sales skills on people that they already know,
first. Then once some confidence in those skills is built, it's easier
to approach people who are acquaintances or unknown alto-
gether. By starting with turning friends into customers, it becomes
easier to turn customers into friends.

That being said, it's also important to recognize that not everyone
is a prospect. Rather than trying to give your pitch to anyone near
you, it's important to figure out if it's a good idea to give the pitch
to the person at all. There's no magical way to do this, successful
distributors just build relationships with as many people as they
can, and if they recognize someone as a potential prospect, they
just know. They've learned what things to look for in a prospect,
such as an interest in the industry or mention of a similar product.
By waiting until a conversation or relationship naturally leads to
discussion of the product, a distributor can avoid being labeled as
an annoying salesman, but instead be considered a helpful distributor of a health product.

Another incredible way to be successful is to leverage online networks. More and more network marketing professionals are using their online networks to accelerate their sales, as it's been shown that 50% of prospects will respond to instant message or email conversation about the opportunity to get involved in the network marketing industry.

A little over a year ago I developed an abscess on my gum line. It looked almost like a large blister on my gum line. After having it for about 6 months I finally decided to go to the dentist, who said he hadn't ever seen anything like it. However, he wasn't sure if it was something that would require a root canal or if it was an issue with my gums, so he referred me to a specialist. I never went. To be truthful, life was too busy...the abscess didn't hurt....and I would have had to pay a somewhat significant out of pocket amount to go to the specialist. I figured I'd just "deal" until it started to hurt.

Fast forward several months...I started drinking the Organo Gold Black coffee on occasion. Then I started to take the Spores on a daily basis. Within a week of taking the Spores, my abscess seems to have disappeared. I had it for about 15 months without any signs of it going away...only to rub my tongue over it after a week on the Spores to find my gums were smooth. I suppose it could be a coincidence.

Dawn M, Thornton, CO

During my investigation of Organo Gold, I ran into a key leader. I did not want him to be the only voice in this book, so I am changing his name so no one will feel I am promoting him. But I thought I would include my meeting with him in this chapter.

I flew to Toronto, Canada, to meet with Mark Davies. He and I met in the large and modern main Toronto Library, on Yonge Street, in a vibrant part of the city's downtown core. There was a coffee shop attached to the library, and Mark disappeared from our table, and quickly returned bearing two glasses of steaming hot water. Offering me any of a variety of Organo beverages, we got to know each other over two delicious lattes.

Not only were they delicious, but we saved about $12 from the price of two lattes in any other downtown coffee shop.

I wanted to meet with Mark, because he was someone who had built his team all over the world, without leaving America (or Canada). His background was accounting, and he was retired when he first heard of Organo Gold. I asked Mark what really caught his attention, because few people at his age, and with his background, rolled up their sleeves and start into the MLM game.

He told me 'it was the fact that his sponsor had become a millionaire within 3 years and with no previous Network Marketing Profession experience prior to OG'.

Mark went on, 'I was also fortunate enough to meet with Master Distributor Shane Morand. He showed me how much OG had grown, yet, with respect to the size of the coffee and wellness market, how OG had barely scratched the surface. There was plenty of opportunity based on the facts that were laid out by Shane and my sponsor.'

Mark saw clear documented 'evidence' showing OG growing 100 times its size. The fact that there are many people involved in OG that never had previous experience as professional networkers really made the decision for Mark to join.

"Look at these major factors," says Mark, "OG has captured the 5 Fastest Growing Industries today. Health & Wellness, Home based Business, Weight Loss, Internet marketing, and of course Coffee, one of the world's most consumed beverages. So what we have here is the ability to capitalize on all these industries at the same time. The brilliance behind this is added 100% organically grown Ganoderma Lucidum in all the products, why? Because people already know how to drink coffee, the fact of the matter is that when they drink Organo Gold coffee, tea or hot chocolate they are getting healthy!"

I sit back and take another sip of my Organo latte. So does Mark. He looks down at his coffee and says "I will not drink any other coffee but Organo's."

Prior to joining Organo Gold, Mark drank percolated coffee. He revealed to me how much he suffered from acid reflex because of that coffee and had to permanently take medication to fight it down. Today he is off his meds and feels great. He looks, talks, walks with an energy of a 30 year old, and looks like he's in his late forties, yet he is over 60. He says he has more energy now and I can believe it just watching him maneuver his way through the busy library full of young students. In his view, he is drinking the finest, tastiest, and healthiest gourmet coffee available.

Turing to the business now, I ask Mark how Organo is different from the other network marketing companies that people have tried to interest him in over the years, product aside.

He tells me that one of the major differences is the fact that Organo is a vertically integrated company that controls the financial and ethical facilities of one of the world's largest Ganoderma producers. It's recognized internationally for its patented cultivation and preparation method of the leading brand of Certified Organic Ganoderma, now the world's largest Ganoderma facility. He feels that vertical integration with the supply side is not the only reason that Organo is an amazing business, but that there are a few key additional factors.

Mark knows a lot about the management side of big business from his accounting background. This is an area that most distributors ignore at their peril, as few have spent time on the management side of big business. Mark had. He tells me that the Organo management group has proven themselves time and time again. They have taken the company to the pinnacle of success in a relatively short period of time rivalling all other companies in this sector, becoming, throughout the world, the number one in terms of momentum growth, and to have produced the highest earners the profession has ever witnessed.

There is one more major factor that Mark reminds me about, and that is the fact that Organo Gold has the first ever exclusive collaboration with the Napoleon Hill Foundation. Nearly every networker is given a copy of Think and Grow Rich at one time in their business career. Napoleon Hill could be considers the unofficial trainer for every MLM distributor in the world.

The Napoleon Hill Foundation and its renowned World Learning Center and produced an exclusive Organo Gold edition of the millionaire makers' best-selling book, Think and Grow Rich. This alone is a testament that Organo Gold is much more than a coffee company, it is a personal development company.

I can't deny that Organo has been busy transforming lives of so many people, with unseen financial compensation and lifestyle changes. From cars to trips and recognition, all made possible because of the 'Simple System' in place that allows everyone to win big. Mark adds, "There is no guess work with Organo Gold, what we are doing absolutely works."

Chapter 10 – How Income is Earned with Organo Gold

So now that the powerful health benefits of Ganoderma are known, product lines have been discussed, and network marketing has been explained, the next topic of discussion is the kind of money that can be made through Organo Gold. In short, the potential earning with this company is incredible. There are 7 ways to earn money! How many ways are there to make money in the corporate world? One? Maybe two? With Organo Gold, not only will you be earning active income, but passive, as well.

The first way to make money is with retail profits. These retail sales are the foundation of the Organo Gold Opportunity. Selling the products to retail customers when you buy them for wholesale prices allows for generous profits of up to 100% that can be paid daily or weekly.

Second, there is a Fast Track Bonus that allows a new distributor to start making money right away on Organo Gold Promotional Product Packs. A distributor can earn up to $150 on each pack, with no limits on the amount of packs that can be sold. This income is paid out on a weekly basis.

Next up is the Dual Team Bonus that pays you to grow your network of distributors working under you. By building, leading, and motivating two business teams, an Organo Gold distributor can potentially earn up to $50,000, which would be paid out on a weekly basis, as well.

Whenever I drink regular coffee I get the shakes/jitters and can feel my heart racing. I'm currently 40 years old and even in my early 20's, if I had a cup of coffee to try and stay awake, I would still be falling asleep at my desk at work, but my heart would be beating FAST!, pounding. After drinking the Organo Gold coffee black, latte, or mocha I do get an energy boost but without the shakes/jitters or racing heart. Also I notice no 'coffee breath' afterward.

Todd H, Canada

There's also a Unilevel Bonus that is the heart of residual income. A distributor receives bonuses from product orders and reorders generated by his entire group, going up to nine levels deep. This income is paid out monthly and is earned without any additional effort. Once members have been recruited and gotten up to speed on how Organo Gold works and what products are offered, this income will come in passively for as long as these "downline" distributors remain with the company. In addition, there's the added bonus of getting residual income not only from those directly recruited by a distributor, but also those recruited by recruits, and so on, for nine levels of recruitment.

There's additional incentive to develop a personal team, as a percentage of the Unilevel Matching Bonus can be earned by Personally Sponsored Distributors. This, too, goes several levels deep and is paid monthly.

Becoming an Organo Gold Leader comes with additional bonuses such as a four generation Generational Bonus that is for qualified sapphire distributors and above. This part of the bonus is paid out monthly.

Lastly, the ultimate reward is the Global Bonus Pool, which allows a distributor to share in 3% of the Total Worldwide Unilevel commissionable volume by reaching above and beyond one's dreams. This bonus is earned monthly but paid quarterly and is really something to reach for.

As it should be clear, there are almost endless opportunities to earn money with Organo Gold. Obviously getting started is the most challenging part, but once a distributor becomes comfortable with relationship building and how to promote the product line, success is nearly inevitable. Once that comfort level has been reached, it's just a matter of time before a large "downline" network is recruited so that residual incomes can be earned and bonuses can be qualified for.

I noticed that every day in the afternoon I had to have a 20-minute nap just to make it through the rest of the day at work, I was gaining weight and losing my motivation in my job. Seemed like the same thing every day going on for months into years. After I was introduced to Organo Gold and I started using the products, I noticed after a couple of months drinking the beverages and using the capsules I wasn't needing my afternoon nap anymore. Last time on my scale I actually lost 13 pounds, I found myself more focused and had more motivation in my life to do things that I would have never thought I could do before Organo Gold. I'll be an Organo Gold customer for life now, I haven't felt better or more alive in years.

Steve T, Loveland, Colorado

While there are many methods of earning money with network marketing, there is absolute nothing better than the Binary Pay option that Organo Gold utilizes for its representatives. Binary pay is the best because it offers far greater potential of earning the highest profits; the money that you really came to make.

Since the concept of binary pay deals with twos, i.e. getting two people in your frontline, two in your downline and so on and so forth, you can build your business much quicker with the method, as well as double, triple and even quadruple your profits tremendously.

And, with binary pay, you can even reenter your business and earn from your downline if you happen to max out at the top, giving you even better chances of getting earning more money from work you did in the past. With a good frontline you can make a tremendous amount of money, even if you are two or three levels down in the line, all thanks to the binary pay plan.

The binary pay option is used by Organo Gold as well as many well-known network marketing companies and is considered one of the fairest compensation plans in network marketing. When you begin your Organo Gold business you will understand why this is the pay plan that will keep you a success.

I'm 37 years old, and I have been a long distance runner for over 12 years now. I'm always working hard to improve my performance and better my race times. I'm also a nurse, so I'm constantly looking for ways to maintain a high level of health. When I was introduced to Organo Gold I was intrigued but skeptical at first. I'm not a coffee drinker so I chose to try the spore capsules instead. I noticed in the first week that I had more energy, I could think clearer and felt more productive in general. After taking the spores for 6 weeks or so I ran a 7 mile race - this race has a quite challenging course. It was a race I had competed in for many years previously. This year, even though I hadn't been training as much as usual, I beat my personal record and I finished about 10 minutes faster than I had expected remember, I hadn't been training as hard as usual. I was excited but curious how I had finished so quickly - then I realized that the only thing new in my life was the Organo Gold spores. And from a medical perspective I feel strongly that these products are effective at helping me cleanse my body of toxins and improve my overall general health. I don't usually like taking pills or too many supplements - I try to get all my necessary nutrients from healthy foods. But I feel that Organo Gold offers healthy properties that other supplements cannot. Thank you Steve for introducing these products to me and I look forward to experiencing more health benefits from Organo Gold.

Danette L, Colorado

Chapter 11 The New Wave of Network Marketing that Organo Gold is Leading

As we just mentioned, once you are comfortable with your product line and the Organo Gold company, success is inevitable if you are willing to put forth the effort. The only thing left for you to do is promote the product line and the business opportunity that awaits. We've already talked about the tremendous growth of network marketing, as well as the massive incomes that are produced with it. Now let's take a look at how you can implement the very best skills into your Organo Gold business and find the success you've been dreaming of.

Being successful with network marketing isn't something that only a select few are cut out for. Anyone in the whole world can be successful at network marketing if they are only willing to listen and learn. You may think you know what it takes to market Organo Gold, but what you learn might surprise you. Network marketing has changed over the past few years, offering a greater opportunity for men and women to promote their product and spread the word about what they have to offer. The Internet has arrived, and with it you can help obtain all of your dreams with Organo Gold.

If you are asking how the Internet has impacted the way that you utilize network marketing, have you considered that more than 1.6 billion people browse the Internet on a daily basis? These individuals are all in search of different things, some there to shop, others there to find arts and crafts projects or to listen to music. And then there are those who are online in search of a business opportunity.

Since I have been taking the Organo Gold Spore Power I no longer have the back pain I use to have on a daily basis. I currently have no pain. I know the Spore Power is real because I ran out for a few days awaiting a shipment to arrive and my body spoke to me the whole time. And it wasn't nice when it is that time of the month instead of taking over the counter meds I now take Organo Gold Spore Power Powder Capsules. They work great!

I was sick to the point I couldn't even get out of bed. I took 3 Organo Gold Grape Seed Oil extract capsules 3 days in a row and no over the counter meds and I was back on my feet like nothing happened. At night I drink the Hot Chocolate and I sleep like a baby. It's the best sleep ever!!!

Raven T, Miami

There are actually many people who use the Internet to help themselves find a business opportunity. They are looking to find something that really sales them from the beginning, something they, too, feel confident in taking the chance with. Think about yourself when you first began network marketing. This means that having your name and your opportunity out in the virtual world is a must if you really want to be successful. With millions of people out there searching for such opportunities, you have the land of opportunity to take your Organo Business to new heights. It is certainly more than possible, as proof with the many others who have succeeded and are making over $50,000 per month with Organo Gold.

The Internet can help you promote your product in ways you never thought possible. You can promote the business opportunity with Organo Gold as well, working to quickly build a nice downline and more profits. The numerous methods of promoting your business are endless, and if you are willing to put in the time and the effort, the Internet could help you see those dreams of making it big come true for you.

One of the biggest things to hit the Internet is social media. Those popular sites like Facebook, Twitter etc. make it possible to connect with friends, family, business associates and fans from all across the world, and they're not just reserved for the teens and the kids. With nothing more than an Internet connection and a bit of time you could really make MLM marketing work for you with the use of social media sites. You can easily build a great line of interested people in your product with the use of these sites. But, as we said, it does take work, effort and a commitment. You cannot start utilizing social media and then fall out of it. You must make the commitment to make social networking work for your Organo Gold business.

Organo Gold has allowed me to drink coffee once again. Regular coffee caused "vice-like" headaches that would creep up on me in the early morning hours. I would need more and more coffee during the day to keep my headaches at bay. With Organo Gold coffee I can enjoy one cup of coffee in the morning without getting a headache the next day.

Traci T, MA, RD, CLT Colorado

It is estimated that more than 1.5 million people visit a social media site on a daily basis, spending at least 15 minutes on with each visit they make. If you make your business a part of the media world, there is a good chance many of those people will have the opportunity to learn what you have to offer. If you have a bit of persuasion and creativity, you can really take off with the Internet and social media working on your side.

Using the Internet and social media can help you easily gain an impressive Organo Gold downline as well as massive sales of the product. As we have already mentioned there are a multitude of ways that you can use the Internet and social media to help you build and expand on your business. If you are willing to put forth the effort you really can have the success. There is no easier way to get to the top; but it takes your desire and need to succeed.

Getting yourself familiarized with social media can help you quickly earn a great amount of money every single month with Organo Gold. There are already many Organo Gold representatives who have begun utilizing social media and the Internet to market their business and you must jump in the boat to stay ahead of the game. Many of those are on the top of the program, earning figures of $50,000 and more every single month. How wonderful would that be? The thing is, this isn't something that you have to sit and dream for. You need to reach for it, and you can be one of those people making the figures that really make sense.

If you thought that social media sites were only for teenagers and the younger generation, it is time to revamp your way of thinking. Businesses around the world are thanking such sites for their success. More and more everyday social media sites cater their websites to those who operate businesses, and this is great news for you! Without the web and social media networking sites many business owners would not have succeeded. As a matter of fact, there are many businesses that are based entirely online without a retail store or a location! Amazon is one that comes to most of us. You know they could not succeed if it weren't for the Internet!

I lost 12 pounds within the 1st month of drinking the Organo Gold coffees and I've been able to keep the weight off.

More importantly, I have asthma and allergies and I usually take Singulair and Allegra year-round. I ran out of pills and hadn't had a chance to refill my prescriptions. When this happens, my body knows I have stopped taking the pills and I start wheezing and the allergies get worse. I started drinking the coffees about a 2 months ago and since then, I have not had to take any Allegra, Singulair or any other allergy medicine.

Shonja M, California

First things first. You should familiarize yourself with all of the top social media networking sites out there. Chances are you will feel a bit overwhelmed when you begin doing this, as there are just so very many of them out there. However, you've probably heard of many of them unless you've been in a cloud somewhere and this can help you choose the most popular sites that will help you gain the most exposure and benefit you in the best ways.

Facebook is one of the most popular of all of the social media sites. They have members from all across the world and offer a number of solutions to those who own small businesses. You can easily create a page for your business where you are free to tell the world about your business and the unique opportunity that you have. Of course you will need to promote your page in order to begin gaining popularity. The first way this can be achieved is by inviting friends and family to join you on the site. You should also post a tag to your Facebook page on your website as well as your blog. Use promotional tools and businesses (also found on Facebook) to help promote your page. Once you begin building the likes and the followers you can then begin promoting your business opportunity and the delicious beverages that it also offers. Facebook offers a multitude of ways in which this can be done.   You can post photos and videos, status updates and more on Facebook while also interacting with customers. This social media site gives you the chance to talk one on one with potential business partners and customers. When you leave them with an impression they'll spread the word. Quickly you can find yourself successful and enjoying the ease or promotion with Facebook.

Of course Facebook is not the only social media website out there. There are tons of others and it is a good idea to get yourself involved with as many of those as you realistically can. Some people may use only one site, and you might also find that some are better at promoting than the other. Popular sites that Organo Gold members often find success with include Twitter, YouTube, LinkedIn and Instagram. Each of these sites are known around the world with millions of members whom are all active. Many of those people are interested in leading a healthy lifestyle or making money. Now it is time to pounce.

Twitter is one of those sites that should also be considered when you are trying to make your Organo Gold business work. Twitter also sees millions of people visiting the site every single day. Here you have the chance to say what you want to say in 150 characters or less. It seems like a tight space, but you can really make a difference in the exposure that your business sees with these small tidbits. Make it interesting and make it count. Ensure that you are using hashtags at the end of your statement. Hashtags make it easy for other people on Twitter to find you. This is, of course, what you want to do.

I have had an amazing past seven years; let me start by telling you what has happened to me. I went on a business trip to Saint Louis, on the way out there I was bitten by a mosquito which in turn gave me the West Nile Virus. I didn't know it and continued to work there for two weeks. The virus moved to my brain making it swell. The swelling left a scar which caused me to start having seizures. I was having nine Grand Mal seizures a day; Grand Mals are the most severe form of seizures, your entire body goes into convulsions. Not very pleasant for me or those around me. Three years ago I had brain surgery to remove that scar.

After the surgery I still had to remain on the medication, if I missed a pill I would start to feel as if I was about to go into a seizure. I actually did have a seizure after my surgery which was a very scary and emotional experience. September 26, 2008 Organo Gold came into my life, after about two weeks on the product I drank the latte I realized that I had forgotten to take a couple of my pills, and I didn't feel any seizure symptoms. So, I decided to test the coffee a little further. I intentionally didn't take my pills for three days. No seizures. Then I went a week. No seizures. Two weeks, a month, two months. It has now been nine months and I haven't taken any of my seizure medication. The only thing that I have changed is I drink a cup of Organo Gold coffee or tea every day. I feel great and am very grateful that Organo Gold came into my life.

Jesse M, Denver, Colorado

It is recommended that YouTube be one of the choices in social media sites that you select when you are ready to help your business explode. If you are not already familiar with YouTube, it is a video sharing site that allows members to upload videos of any length, on any topic. Other users can watch the video as well as like, comment and share with others using other social media sites. Watching a video has power with it, and when you are looking to add individuals to your downline while also increasing sales of a product, there is no better way to make it happen than with the use of a video.

There are a number of ideas that can be utilized in the creation of your video. As long as you keep the video interesting and informative, as well as 3 to 5 minutes in length you are on your way to a wonderful way of promoting your Organo Gold business. Your video can talk about the health benefits of the beverages; 10 reasons why you should drink them. Or, if you are more on the recruiting end of things right now, create a video showing why this is the perfect time to get in on the Organo Gold business or how to easily make money. As we said the possibilities for a video are endless.

Keep the videos interesting. Make certain that you take the time to plan the video well ahead so it is professional and represents you as the expert you want to be known as. At the end of the video ensure that you direct people where to go to begin the wonderful opportunity that you have presented to them. Usually this will direct people to your website. You can also post this link in the written summary section underneath the video.

Just over 4 years ago I went to my Doctor and discovered that my health was at risk. I started the regimen of working out and eating right; however nothing really changed. After more visits to the doctor, my medical team decided to put me on medication that was intended to help with these health issues. The medication was somewhat successful, but ultimately came with other side effects. Mid to late September of last year I was introduced to "Healthy Coffee". I beginning drinking at least one cup per day and one capsule of Ganoderma in the morning. Since then I am no longer dealing with the health risks from before and I am also no longer required to take the prescribed medication

James H, Denver, Colorado

Of course there are tons of other social media sites that you should make yourself a part of. When you do the best of possibilities will come your way and you can count on getting your business a successful start. Create as many social media accounts for your networking as possible. Be sure that you do not overwhelm yourself with sites, however, as you do need to keep them updated. However, with the popularity of social media, it never hurts to make your presences known in all of the different manners possible.

Remember, as with any business, things are always changing and you want to be on top of those changes. Keep your pages updated regularly, and always make them interesting and enticing to the customers. This will help capture a broader audience. Remember, they want to connect with you. Update photos regularly, post new statuses, respond to all comments that are left. Get personal and you can get successful with your business.

So, social media really makes that much of an impact on your business? You bet that it does! When you utilize social media networks it really presents you with opportunity to connect with other people on a personal level. People want to connect with humans, not a business. They want to know they are making the right choices, that they can be successful and that you will stand behind them every step of the way. These sites make it more than possible for you to connect to people in this manner.

This is something that is even more important when you are with a business such as Organo Gold. Part of being successful with the company involves helping those who are also in your downline. You should have a combination of individuals within the downline, each with something positive to bring to the group.

When an individual sees they can connect with you, they understand how much more they can be successful in the business and are that much more likely to join you.

Organo Gold businesses can also use social media to help them promote their business and their products. You can advertise specials on social media sties, as well as place links back to your website or to other information that you want your customers to see. It is a good idea to promote yourself on the sites, but do it in a non-threatening manner, meaning do not focus all of your attention on selling yourself. It is a good idea to post links that back up any statements that you are make concerning Organo Gold, the money that can be made or the benefits of the tea and coffee. Post humors updates and photos, and always keep things as interesting and as engaging for your followers as possible. You want them to love your page and recommend it to others. This means you need to give them what they love.

I never went to the restroom regularly, I actually didn't realize that it was abnormal as no one really talks about it. I as grew older I realized that it's not normal to only use the restroom every three or four days. When Organo Gold came into my life at first it cleaned me out... When they say it detoxifies you, they aren't kidding. Because of the detox I have been able to lose 23 pounds – a great side effect. Now, after nine months on the product coffee, tea, and caps I use the restroom every day. I feel happier and healthier.

Jet E, Denver, Colorado

When the Internet is used to help market your Organo Gold products you can count on gaining a large number of customers and believers in your product. There will be many who will be interested in what you have to say and want in on the opportunity to make a great profit themselves. This is true whether you are just starting out or if you have already established yourself as a reputable Organo Gold business owner. All that it takes to do this is to build that personal connection with those around you.

When you use the Internet to help spread the word about your business you are doing all that you can to reach the largest possible audience. With multiple avenues that you can access to promote your business online, you are certainly going to be able to find the success that you have been looking for. Understanding how to market Organo Gold will ensure that you are seeing those six-figure payouts you've been dreaming of!

With the web you can promote your business in many different ways, utilizing all 7 of the money-making opportunities Organo Gold brings your way. There are many ways that the Internet can help you promote and network your product as well as turn others interested in earning a profit into your world in addition to social media. Basically, the Internet is the world of limitless opportunity. When you use these many different methods it is more than possible to make the kind of money worth talking about. That is, after all, the ultimate goal in place when you begin working with Organo Gold.

Marketing Organo Gold online is not difficult to do, however you must be able to establish the methods that will work best for your needs and avoid the rest. There are far too many methods of net-work marketing to try them all, and attempting to do so will only cause you frustration. Of course you will also find that not all of those marketing methods are suitable for Organo Gold products either. It is certainly necessary to promote your business, but it can quickly become overbearing and tiresome if you are trying to do too much. Ensure that you examine all of your available net-work marketing options and familiarize yourself with them. If you feel they'll provide you the best results without the hassle, try your luck. It is also a good idea to talk to those higher up in the totem pole than you are. Certainly they'll be able to provide you with many a useful lesson, tips, ideas and information. They, too, started where you are at and have exceeded all limits and expec-tations and reached new heights within the program.

I've been drinking all of the Organo beverages since Dec. 2008. I would like to start off saying that from my first cup of Organo Gold Gourmet Black - my favorite - I have noticed much more energy and stamina. Also, I started using the Organo Gold cap-sules in May 2009 and the tremendous differences in my life that these caps have brought for me are fantastic. My eyes have been blood shot red for years and after taking these caps my eyes have cleared up very noticeably. I've also been getting lots of com-ments on my skin. All thanks to our wonderful G3 soap.

Ernest H, Aurora, CO

We've already discussed how powerful using in social media is for your business and now we will look at the many other ways you can use the Internet to promote your business. All of this may seem like a lot of work, but in the end all of the time and effort that you put will really pay off and you can be successful. You will see results as you go along, with more and more people who want to sign up and start making money selling this amazing health tea and coffee. The more people you recruit, the more marketing that   you do, the more profitable and successful your business will be.

A secret tip that many Organo Gold members use to promote their products and business opportunity is an autoresponder. An autoresponder automatically responds to messages that are sent to an email box. They can be simpler they can be complex depending on the email/offer that you are using. One thing is for certain, they really make life easy when it is time to market, especially when your promoting begins to show results. You can easily create an auto-respond message that is thought provoking, convincing and gets the parties interested and ready to do what you are doing. If you are using an email marketing campaign, or otherwise offering a special offer for all who respond for more information, this is certainly a good idea that you should consider.

My husband Bryan had been having trouble sleeping and just didn't look well. He is a diabetic and has been on pain medication for the last 5 years for migraines. After the first day of drinking the Organo Gold Black Coffee he slept through the night. After the first week he said he noticed he had more energy and just felt better. He did experience some mild detoxing during the first week. Friends and family also have noticed how much better he is looking. Before drinking the Organo Gold coffee his color wasn't good. His eyes had a glazed over appearance. He has been able to cut back on his pain medication and hopes to be able to get off them all together. He continues to comment on how much better he is feeling.

I had been suffering for about 5 months every day and night from terrible pain on the bottom of my right foot. I drank my first Organo Gold Mocha in the evening then went to bed. I woke up the next morning and got out of bed and was totally shocked to find No Pain in my foot! I said out loud "Holy Cow what's in that stuff?" It's been a little over two weeks since I started drinking Organo Gold drinks and the pain has not returned.

I also have noticed more energy and when I wake up in the morning I feel well rested and find it easier to get out of bed, and I am not a morning person!

Terri and Bryan H, Albany, Oregon

Creating lists is of the most importance when you are seeking interested parties in your business. This is known as prospecting and is the first step of a powerful combination of marketing your Organo Gold business. Prospecting is the art of pulling the customers in to see who is interested and what you can do to get them on in the door and seal the deal. You need to target business minded individuals who have shown an interest on your product or the types of product that you are offering. Those who have also shown an interest in MLM and business opportunities are great for you to build your list with. These individuals are much more likely to respond to what you have to offer. Just imagine yourself sitting inside of a crowded room with a bunch of people talking about the FOREX market, something you have 0 interest in. No matter what these individuals said you aren't going to be any more interested in it. The same goes for your Organo Gold business. You do not want to waste your breath or your time on those who could care less about what you are offering or the business opportunity. For this reason it is essential that you target those who are interested in what you have to offer.

There are a multitude of ways you can find those who are interested in Organo Gold, including through the placement of advertisements (this can be done both off and online,) newsletter signups and eBook giveaways, mailing lists, as well as many other methods. Make sure that you take this small step to gain followers who are really interested in what you are offering to them. This makes it easier to see positive results in a much quicker amount of time.

Take a look at some of the best ways to market Organo Gold on the World Wide Web. Those already in on the Organo Gold success have used these marketing methods and have seen the best of results. So can you if you are willing and ready.

Email Marketing: Email marketing is becoming more and more popular among small business owners who seek to enrich their business. The benefit of email marketing to Organo Gold is numerous, as you can attain a list of interested parties to send out mailings to. Your mailings are sent directly to the recipient's email box. The possibilities are endless in email marketing. Use it to notify customers of a sale that you have going on, the money that is being made with Organo Gold or any other special offers you want the world to know about.

Attaining an email marketing list is easy to do. First, attain interested parties email addresses through free newsletter sign-ups, eBook giveaways or other special promotions. In your advertising to get an individual to sign up, be sure to promote your product in a positive manner without revealing the secret. It is at this point you can add them to your email list, as long as they have agreed to be contacted by you.

Done correctly, Organo Gold business owners can see positive results using email marketing to help grow their business in substantial numbers.

Article Marketing: It may be hard to understand how article marketing can help you build a downline or customers wanting to order your product, however, you should not miss out on the fabulous opportunity that article marketing offers to you.

According to surveys, most people using the Internet are searching for information on a product they wish to buy, or browsing products in a specific category to purchase. Did you catch the first part of that? They want information. By creating articles targeting Organo Gold, the benefits, the profits that can be made, the ease of making those profits, etc., you can really increase the likelihood of seeing interested individuals at your website.

I am twenty years old, and I am in love. I am in love with the Organo Gold products. The results that I have experienced since I began drinking the Organo Gold healthier coffee have completely changed the course of my future. When I was a freshman in high school I missed almost half of that school year because I was ill.

I was in and out of doctor's offices, laid up in bed, had my blood work tested and retested, and I couldn't find a doctor that could explain why I was sick or what I had. Even though they couldn't tell me what exactly was making me sick the doctors wanted me to try a couple of different medications to see if any of them might work. I didn't want to play Russian roulette with medication, so I decided to just deal with the pain. I thought that I was going to live my life being sick. My life changed when, after two weeks of drinking the amazing Organo Gold products, I noticed that I wasn't feeling sick. Then, after two months, I noticed that I was feeling great!

It has been over seven months now since I had my first cup of healthier coffee, and the last seven months have been the longest I have gone without being sick for the last five years. I would never have guessed that God would bless me with a cup of coffee, but I am sure glad he did.

Casey N, Loveland, Colorado

Article marketing is simple. All you do is create an article based around your products and services. The above possibilities are all great ideas for your article, however you can create something based on any information that you wish to provide. As long as it is well-written, informative and offers the reader value, it can certainly make a great article for a directory.

When creating your articles, be sure to focus on the keywords you have chosen to market your product, and ensure that the end of all articles contain a quick snippet about yourself, your business and a link back to your website where they can learn more information or join the money-making opportunity, or even make a purchase. Your articles should be well-written and professional, so if you are not comfortable creating such an article, consider using a professional writer. It is worth the small amount of money that you will spend.

Once this has been done, submit the article to an article directory. They'll need to approve your article in most circumstances. This can take up to 7 days, so be patient. Since there are many article directories out there, it is a good idea to create a few different articles for each. This will certainly help you gain more exposure! Many article directories are free, although it is important that you know there are also paid article directories.

Create a Website: This is the most important thing that you can do to build your business on the web. With your own website customers can go straight to the source for their information, to join or to make a purchase, eliminating all of the clicks and time.

Creating a website isn't the easiest thing in the world to do, but it isn't hard, either. If you have just a bit of creativity and the drive to succeed you will easily be able to create a website that creates a lasting impression on all who visit. It will also take you a little bit of time, so make sure that you have created a time that you can devote just to the creation of your site. With the possibility of so many people seeing it, devoting this attention is a must to ensure that you create something that is enjoyable for all who visit.

I love what the Organo Gold products have done for me. I have been going through menopause for almost ten years, and during the last ten years I have not slept through the night. It was hard to function on even daily tasks when I didn't get any sleep. After drinking the healthy latte I slept through the night for the first time in ten years. I not only sleep better, I have more energy and better focus. I now have a cup of coffee every night before bed.

Deanna N, CO

Your website should be captivating and interesting. It should contain lots of useful information concerning the things the audience really wants to know about the beverages, the money they can make and more. How much money can be made? How much time must be spent into the program? How are the coffees and teas beneficial to the health? All of these things are important to put on your site. You can include this information in a FAQ section if you like, although it is good to highlight at least a couple of the benefits on the home page.

Also remember that you should create an easy to use site that is beneficial and plentiful to those who visit. Nothing will scare someone away faster than a site that is hard to use. Make sure you give them what they want.   Make the site simple for someone ready to join your marketing team as well as for those who want to test out the products for themselves. This is the only way to make the money that you want to make!

Always optimize your website for SEO purposes, and utilize key-words that are highly searched for and relevant to what you are selling or promoting. When you optimize your website it is more than possible to get yourself noticed by twice or three times the number of people as you would have originally.

Along with the creation of your website, you can place backlinks on other sites, use article directories to link back to your website and even advertising on other websites. Be certain that you consider all of these options to market your business to an international platform. All of these things are very beneficial when you are looking to get people to visit your website and to set a buzz about the products that you are offering to them. But, again, always make sure that you are utilizing information from that country when you are doing these things.

Thank you for introducing me to the wonderful Organo Gold Latte. As you know I am not a coffee drinker but now I'm an Organo Gold fanatic!!! I have been drinking the latte and taking the spores for about 6 months now. I have suffered from hemiplegic migraines for the past 9 years. These migraines mimic strokes by paralyzing the entire left side of my body and are very painful. I get them every 30 days around "that time of the month". I cannot walk or talk when they come on. They could last anywhere from an hour to 3 days. I've tried all types of meds and they really haven't worked.

Once I started drinking this healthier coffee and taking the capsules the migraines "coincidentally" stopped!!! I no longer have to miss a class or work due to these horrible migraines. My quality of life has changed for the better!!!!

Remeshian P, Denver, CO

This is also something you should do only when you've built a website you are confident it. It is a good idea to have someone look over the finished product before you place it live. You do not want customers to get the wrong impression of you, even for a millisecond. While it needs to be SEO optimized, it should be created for the reader with this information kept in mind, not the other way around.

Blogging: If you enjoy writing and sharing experienced with others, consider blogging. Many already in the Organo Gold program use blogging as a marketing platform, and so should you! There are endless possibilities of creating your blog, with many free hosting options as well. WordPress is one of the most popular blogging platforms out there but you can always use the blogging platform of your choice.

When a customer wants to make a purchase, the first thing they want to do is build a personal connection with the brand. When you blog you can certainly connect to your customers on a personal level, as well as extend to them your knowledge, information and expertise. People who enjoy your blog will certainly enjoy what you have to offer. It is certainly a good idea to create a blog to help in your Organo Gold business endeavors.

Make sure that you keep your blogs sweet, simple and interesting. Always leave it open-ended and ask people to participate in discussion about the post that you have made. This is yet another powerful way to engage with your customers, build that important personal connection and help your business grow. As with all of the other methods of marketing your business, this one is very popular as well successful, and should be something that you consider doing. You do not have to be a professional writer, you just need the desire to sell your product and connect with others.

Since I've been drinking Organo Gold, I've lost 10 lbs in about 2 weeks and the coffee gives me stamina and focus when I'm working out.

Derek S, Pearland, Texas

This coffee is AMAZING! I have had 2 Lattes & a Black coffee this morning. My mind is focused. I am exploding with energy, and I am sitting a few inches farther away from my computer screen at work, seeing clearly!

Tim L, Overland Park, KS

There are also a few other things that you should keep in mind when utilizing the above-mentioned methods of marketing Organo Gold to the world. When you use these tips together with the information you can count on getting the downline you want and the customers to build the success. Take a look at these things that are essential in maintain a great following with your Organo Gold business.

Seek Business-Minded Individuals: Those who have previously shown an interest in opening their own business, network marketing or MLM should be targeted when you are creating any type of marketing campaign. Those individuals are much more likely to show interest in what you are offering to them. When you seek business-minded individuals you are saving yourself time, headache and hassle while helping to quickly build a massive downline. They want it, you've just got to sell it to them.

Learn how to be Effective: The most important thing that you should do when marketing your business is learn how to be effective in all of your ventures. You can use social media all day long and not see any results, just as you can use the other methods and see nothing. You must learn how to get down to business, how to do these things and attain effective results. Evaluate the results that you are receiving from the various ways you are marketing. If you are really not seeing any response, chances are you aren't doing something right and should make improvements. Look at the methods that are working to see what you could potentially change to get results.

Create Urgency: Creating urgency in joining, in becoming one of the most successful marketers of the Organo Gold product is the most important thing that you can do. Let people know how critical it is they join in on the revolution before the secret is out. The more motivating and influential you can get it, the better.

I suffer from chronic bronchitis four times a year. A friend shared a cup of Organo Gold Green Tea with me on a Wednesday. I drank a cup in the morning and one at night for 3 days straight. By Saturday, I sang at a wedding and the coughing stopped. By Monday, the majority of the congestion was gone. My normal gestation period for bronchitis is 2-4 weeks. With this product, it didn't even last a week.

Selina P

It takes Time: Time is an essential part of most any task that you attempt. You will not build a strong downline overnight, nor will you sell your products like magic when you first begin. Learning that you need patience is definitely a strong virtue when you are engaging in an Organo Gold MLM business. The average Organo Gold member took approximately four to five months to begin seeing their results.

Once you use these strategies to market Organo Gold you will be able to earn income around the clock. Even as you sleep the systems and strategies you have in place are working to promote the amazing business opportunity and the wonderful coffee and tea that you have available. That is certainly something that you can appreciate when you are looking to make the most possible money with your business.

There are certainly many other things that you can do to promote your business, however these are among some of the best. Remember, social media is king and you need to be a part of it first and foremost, before you do anything else. Everyone uses it and every one can benefit from it, especially those e looking to build an impressive business.

Reach out to both those who want to include healthy products in their lives as well as those who are looking to make a profit. Marketing to each of these individuals is handled in practically all of the same ways, it just requires you to word things differently. In most cases you can sell the product as well as promote the business on the very same platform. But, you may also want to consider creating separate outlets for both of them. This is definitely important when you are advertising. As long as you are able to connect personally with a person it really will not matter what you are trying to do as you will be able to win their hearts over with the great information they can provide to you.

I started drinking Organo Gold not because I wanted, but because my wife switched my favorite brand with a cup of Organo Gold's Gourmet Latte without me even noticing. When she asked me "Honey, how was the coffee?" I responded with "Great as usual honey!" But then I noticed her laughing as if she had done something to the coffee. When she explained to me that I was drinking Organo Gold and the actual benefits it carried, I thought "why not, I'm always drinking coffee anyway, why not make it a healthier choice." One week later and I notice a huge difference in my energy level. From waking up at full speed and slowly running out of steam by 2pm, all of a sudden my energy level is lasting until 6pm, then 8pm. And now I'm pretty much energetic all day! And that's not all. Just like many men out there, we can snore like freight trains running cross country. But even the amount of snoring has dropped, not all together, but my wife is getting a better night's sleep because the decibel level has lowered in our bedroom at night.

Pablo G, USA

Chapter 12 How to build your Network Marketing business internationally without leaving home

Consider this: Marketing your products to an international customer base could help increase your downline percentages and the customers that you have by as much as 45%! The coffee and tea products from Organo Gold are absolutely amazing, offering health benefit after health benefit that people all across the world can enjoy. They are just as interested in owning the best coffee products as those in America and should be available to try those products. They also want to make money and a great opportunity that can help them make the most profits. They should be provided with this opportunity as well. When you take the necessary steps to show these people the magic of Organo Gold you can also help yourself to an array of exciting benefits. How fascinating would it be to add the potential of billions of people being able to join in on the Organo Gold fun and starting the craze in other territories? When those who join you also refer others they are on your downline and this means making profit and more profit. Taking your business international is the best way to do this. Many who are before you in the Organo Gold business have taken their business globally, and it is a good idea that you also join in with these people. The international market is huge, and that means only great things for you.

I received the coffee on January 7th by UPS. I have been on the Organo Gold coffee for 5 days now. I'll admit I am drinking more of it that usual just because it tastes so darn good and my body is actually craving the feeling it is giving me every time I have a cup. These are the results of being back on the coffee for 5 days having 3 coffees a day and taking 1 spore pill:

- *Sleeping soundly*

- *No tossing and turning restless*

- *No more bloating*

- *Waking up refreshed*

- *Acne clearing up*

- *Energy back in full force*

- *Digestive system regular happy bowel movements*

- *Depression gone – I was able to get off my anti-depressant and sleep medication with Organo Gold when I started the product.*

Janet M, USA

As we have already discussed in the previous chapter, the Internet and social media have grown so rapidly over the past few years it is more than possible to do most anything that you can imagine for your business, including market to an international audience. It is definitely one of the best ways to market your Organo Gold products to those who are thousands of miles away. Best of all, you can do this in your pajamas any time of the night or day! Nothing feels better than sitting at home with your favorite pajamas and a comfortable white t-shirt while you work and make more money than you ever could at that 9 to 5. After you begin marketing internationally you will find this your favorite activity every single day!

The key to gaining a large base of international followers is to be persistent and to use all of the tools that are available to you.

There are quite a few things that you can do to gain an international following and it is a good idea to implement as many of those strategies as you can into your life. They will only help you build and grow in your business and that is exactly what you want to do above all else!

While international marketing of a business might have been hard at one point and time, this is no longer the case. As we talked about in the last chapter, the Internet and social media have really made an improvement to the world and changed the way that we do things. You can easily promote Organo Gold to people all across the world and never have to leave your home to do it. There are a multitude of ways that you can do this, both with the web and off. While social media is certainly favored when you want to attain international customers, there are certainly many other ways in which you can profit as well with international marketing. It is a good idea to consider taking your product globally if you want to be as successful as you possibly can be.

Take a look at some of the many ways you can market your Organo Gold business to those on an international level. You will find that every method listed provides a plethora of opportunity for you to create your downline as well as an effective way of gathering customers without a lot of hard work involved. It is simply amazing to have this information as you can do so much for your business, both on sales levels as well as to gaining more customers and more sales of the product. Be sure to utilize as many of the methods for international marketing as possible to attain the best results. They are all proven to be beneficial in the market, as well as things that you may have already learned in the initial process of marketing the product.

I love the fact that I can drink Organo Gold coffee and get the energy boost I need, but it doesn't make me shaky or restless.

Jenny J, Wheaton, Illinois

I drink it at night and feel so rested the next day!

Celia C, Dallas, Texas

First and foremost, the World Wide Web is by far the most valuable tool available to you in the world of network marketing, period. There is no easier, faster way to get information to people far, far away. Nor is there any faster or easier way to market your product to individuals in these faraway lands. If you have access to the Internet you have all that is needed to spread the word about your coffee business in international locations far and wide. You can easily promote the product and the opportunity to individuals anywhere in the world. There is no limit to where you can advertise. Of course, since you are marketing internationally it is important that you do know a little bit of information about the country that you are marketing to before you jump right in. Make sure that it is a country that is at peace with international trade, as well as a country that would allow their residents to participate in such a money making opportunity and that Organo Gold is open there. This is not possible in all countries, but in most.

As we mentioned in the last chapter, the web offers a variety of tools for all Organo Gold business owners who are seeking to make it the best business possible. Again, social media marks the top spot for the best way to market your product to an international audience. Popular US social media sites such as Facebook and Twitter are available for users all across the world and have members from far and wide. As such you can find members scattered on all parts of the world who may very well be interested in what you are offering to them. You can even cater your pages to international territories if you choose, or create a separate page for them. This is all a personal decision, but do keep in mind that you need to maintain all of the sites that you create on a regular basis.

Along with US based social media sites, make sure that you focus your attention to those internationally as well. Since you are taking your products and business across the borders, ensuring that you utilize some of the websites for these other countries is a must. You will find tons of different social media sites that you can become involved with, including Faceparty, CyWorld and Studivz. This mean you can come together with people no matter where your plans for marketing may be. Make sure that you utilize social media whenever you need to boost your downline or add more sales to your order list. You might just be surprised at how well that it works, especially when you take the time to do things the way they should be done.

Since Organo Gold has been in my life, stress has left, and I am more energized…good to have that feeling of accomplishment in all I do!

Barby O, Panama City, Florida

I have all this extra energy and I'm zooming around my office. People have definitely noticed a change in me. When I wake up in the morning, I am smiling because I have slept so well the night before. When people ask me how I am doing, I say WONDERFUL!! Someone asked me why was I so happy and energetic... I had to tell them it was ORGANO GOLD!!!

Deshon T, Grand Blanc, Michigan

There are an assortment of ways that you use social media to benefit you. The ways that you will use vary according to the site that you are using, however, most sites make it possible for you to do a number of things, ranging from posting photos and status updates to listing special offers, promotions or giveaways or even uploading videos. You should use a combination of things on these social media sites to help build your brand and the exposure that you seek for your business. Make sure that you take a look at each site before you begin to see the opportunities that are available on the site before you begin. This will help you create information that is tailored specifically to the site and gain more exposure at the same time.

When you are 'out there' you can expect the people to come making your presence known in the social media world is an essential step in getting where you want to be. Make sure that you are a part of this world.   As you can see there are so many different things that you can do to get the word out about your business and it is a good idea that you use as many of them as possible.

Social media marketing is truly an amazing way to gain custom-ers on international territories and it is by far one of the easiest ways to gain those individuals that you seek to help make your business a great success. Make sure that you use it because you are going to gain more people who are interested in what you have than you could ever imagine. Just as we mentioned about personalizing the connection with your customers in the US, this is also important for you to do when you are looking for interna-tional customers. There are thousands and thousands of people on these sites as well, and they are looking to get what you have to offer them. Other people are using social media to target new business owners and coffee enthusiasts, and you do not want them to get to people before you do.

While social media is very popular, there are many who simply do not use the sites. You do not want to miss out on the oppor-tunity to market your business to them, however, so make sure that you do not stop at social media to advertise your Organo Gold opportunities. There are so many more people out there who need the information that you hold; those that can help you conquer the Global Bonus Pool and sink your hands into the ton of extra money that it offers.   Make sure that you target those individuals as well because you do not want to miss out. You will find the Internet makes it easy to market your business elsewhere in addition to social media. While you do want to focus a great deal of attention to the social media world you should not let this be your sole focus. You will miss out on so much if it is. And that is money that could have been in your pocket. What a loss!

Take a look at some of the many other proven successful ways that you can help spread the word about your marketing busi-ness. Make sure that you research each of the ideas and get a better understanding of how it works and the potential benefits that it can bring to you. It is also a good idea to talk to your sponsor and others in your group to discover if it is something that can be beneficial in the marketing of Organo Gold. We are listing methods that have been used time and time again, often by those with an Organo Gold business, so you will find that most of the ideas are really worth your time.

Make sure that you list your business with major search engines. Google is the most popular, but you shouldn't forget about the other major search engines such as Yahoo, Bing and MSN. When you register your business with the search engines an individual can easily find you within the listing when they search the web for your chosen keywords or business listing title. Doing this is a critical step, as it can really help international customers with limited search options narrow down the selection and target your Organo Gold opportunity.   There is no cost to register your business here, so why not take the time to do it when there is so many potential people who can learn of your presences?

Have you considered placing a Sponsored Ad within a search engine? Those ads that you see above the results in a search engine help you gain exposure quickly. You simply select the keywords that you want your ad to appear under. When someone enters the term of your keyword into a search engine, your results will come up in the sponsored ads. Many people click these ads when they are unhappy with the results the web has provided, as well as when you have a convincing enough tag to attract them to you. Known as pay-per-click advertising, this is a relatively inexpensive methods of marketing and is highly beneficial when looking to recruit people to join you in your Organo Gold opportunity.

Participating in international forums is also another excellent way to bring awareness to your Organo Gold products. These forums can be found with a search of the web and allow you the chance to respond to questions and give your insight. When you participate and leave your remark you can also include a link back to your products. Leaving well educated answers to questions that relate to Network Marketing, coffee/tea and wellness products along with your information is a wonderful chance to not only build your audience but to also provide yourself an expert in the field. Everyone wants to know the person they are working with is knowledgeable in the product they are selling.

Also mentioned in the last chapter, blogging and article directories are also methods of marketing Organo Gold internationally. Take a look at article directories and blog directories that are available in the countries that you wish to market your sales towards. You will find a slew of them no matter which country you look toward, as it is such a popular thing for everyone. Create a few good posts and post, all with your link. Just as the method will help you when you are looking to build your business in the US, these tips will help you grow in the selected country that you are promoting your business with.

Consider creating a website for the country that you wish to promote Organo Gold to. You may even be able to go directly through the OG website to do this. Creating a website will allow individuals to find a place to go to gather all of the information needed to determine whether this is the right opportunity for them. Be sure that you also include links back to you, your email address and other contact information, as well as order forms so that customers who want to place an order can do so. Ensure that you create this website in the language of the other country. This will make it easier for individuals to understand what is being offered to them and make the right business decision.

The website should, of course, be tailored for the reader while also including keywords that are specially chosen for the particular country. The web site should be easy to use as well as informative, helping those who visit understand the information they need but more. You want to convince them that this is the opportunity they've been dreaming of, the ultimate way to live a healthy lifestyle while still enjoying the thing they love, as well as the best way to produce a steady stream of income day by day and week after week.

It is a good idea to go into far more detail about your products than simply advertising them on your website. Make sure that your site includes blogs, photos, testimonials (if they are available,) articles, advice and tips on there as well. Make it interesting for customers, make them want to learn more and help show them that it is an opportunity they cannot pass away. When this information is included you will be seen as an expert and someone that is there to help. This will help more people trust in your and what you are saying, therefore making them much more easy to gain them as a customer in the future.

Another important step to take when you are building your business is to access other virtual tools that are available. Have you considered creating a monthly or weekly newsletter advertising your products and business opportunity? You can create a list and send this information to people as little or as much as you would like. Inside of the newsletter you will should place valuable information that will entice the individual who is reading it. Tailor all of the information to the reader and make it as interesting as you possibly can make it. Always include contact information as well as a small tidbit about yourself and your business so people can contact you when they are ready to being.

This is just one of the many virtual tools out there designed to make it successful for you to build your brand no matter where you aim to target. Make sure that you take a look at all of those tools and utilize those that would be of most benefit to you. There are many available to you at no cost, as well as those that you will need to pay for. If you aren't interested in spending any money, that is okay because the number of free tools is astonishing and just as beneficial as those you would pay to use.

Along with the Internet, you may want consider other methods of marketing your business from home, including with the use of mailers and fliers. These postcards and fliers can contain any and all information that you really want people to know, and there are plenty of individuals who you can send them to. This is another reason that it is important you familiarize yourself with the country you intend to promote your product too. You can send your information to individuals that has been attained from a mailing list, but you can also send it to wellness product business owners who could very well be interested in what you have to offer to them. As you can see there are plenty of ways in which you can use this form of marketing, and it is beneficial that you do so.

The placement of ads is a good idea that can be down from home to help market Organo Gold to an international audience. You can place an ad in any international publication or on any website to help gain exposure to your business. There are so many choices available you can do so much with these ad placements. Consider using newspapers and online newspapers to place your ads. There are also free local sites that you can use to promote your product as well. Ads in newspapers and other publications are relatively inexpensive and ensure that you reach an even broader audience than what you would simply utilizing the services that are available on the web. While millions are online there are many who are not, and with the placement of ads you can ensure that you are reaching these people as well. There is no one that should be left out of the chance to make money and enjoy a great product at the same time and with this you are covering all bases so that no one is left out. Look for publications that are available in the countries that you wish to target. Most will allow you to place your ad and make payment via the World Wide Web. Look for those publications that concentrate on wellness products and/or business opportunities to get the best results from your ad. Also, since there are thousands and thousands of publications that you can choose from, make your choice wisely. Consider readership of the publication as well as the value that your ad will make in that particular publication. It is also a good idea to consider placing more than one ad across several different countries to gain more exposure.

You should also do all that you can to build relationships with others who are in similar or the same industries in these other countries. There are many people in foreign countries that can help you get ahead of the game when they believe in you and the Organo Gold products. It is up to you to make them a believer, but as amazing of products as offered, as well as the potential amount of money that can be made, this should not be difficult at all. Getting to know these people is an absolutely wonderful thing for you to do, and there are many ways this can be done. Take a look at those methods and try your hand. Chances are you will love what these people can do for your business in their country.

It is important that you do keep a few things in mind when network marketing to another country. First, it is essential that you familiarize yourself with their language. It is wrong to assume they'll be able to speak English, because this is not always the case.

Communication is essential when you want to tell someone how amazing the opportunity to make money with Organo Gold really is. If you want to build an international audience, make sure that you can communicate in their language! Even if it is learning just a few words that are critical to your business, make sure that you have this with you. Bear in mind a number of translation services are available as well.

You should also remember to familiarize yourself with the laws and rules and regulations of such a business before you begin. You can be successful only when your downline is successful, and this means complying with all laws, rules and regulations set forth in a particular country. While some laws may be the same in another country as they are in the US, this is not always the case and you do not want to take the chance of doing something that you should not have done and see a lot of trouble brewing in the air. You can make sure that the both of you are successful when you understand what you are getting into when you take your product international. Make sure that you take this needed time to familiarize yourself with the information before you begin.

Marketing to international audiences is not difficult as you can see, and most of this can be contributed to the help the World Wide Web provides. Since coffee and tea are both product that people all across the world enjoy, taking your business across the oceans is a great decision that can certainly help you with more sales. When they discover the amazing health benefits that are also included with the coffee you can certainly expect it to gain even more popularity. Of course those who are on international lands are just as interested in making money with their own business, which can also help you build more people in your downline. International business actually contributes to a great percentage of profits in America, with about 35% of profits coming outside of the states.

Again, just as building your downline and customers in the US took time, it will also take time for this to occur when you are marketing internationally. Always set reasonable expectations for this to happen, as they make it much easier to handle the task of marketing your business.

All of the information listed above has proven successful for those involved with network marketing as well as parties involved with Organo Gold. According to "Entrepreneur" magazine, MLM is one of the fastest ways to make money full or part-time. They also say that the above mentioned tips are those that are most used by those in such a business as well as methods that are proven to work. You have the information and it is up to you to decide what will be done with the information. You can choose to use it and make yourself and your business successful or you can choose to go with the other methods that are not proven to beneficent an MLM business. It is obvious which path you should take. All of the methods listed here are easy enough that anyone can easily do them without any hassle or headache. The results will not take place over night, but with time you will see success.

Marketing your business, whether it is in the US or internationally, is something that you can do when you use all of these tips and this information. But remember, take things one step at a time. You cannot possibly commit to doing all of these things at once, and doing so will do nothing but cause you frustration and to tire out. Little by little increase the marketing strategies that you are using until you have them all. It takes time to grow in your business, just as it takes time to get it all put together. You should not try to jump ahead, move around or skip certain pieces of the puzzle. They must all come together to work as effectively as you would like for them to, but again, it is something that takes time.

Chapter 13 The Bottom Line on Organo Gold and You

The bottom line is that all of these things build your business and your profit and should not be left out of your marketing plan for Organo Gold. As we have said time and time over, the potential to be successful with Organo Gold is there, but it is up to you to make that success. It isn't easy and it isn't going to happen overnight but for those who are up for the challenge and the commitments it is certainly not something that is out of reach either. There is a lot of work involved with being successful. But, as they say, anything worth having will not come easy. When the money starts rolling in you will know that all of your efforts have truly paid off. This can be your future scenario when you piece together all of this information and begin working the Organo Gold program the way it should be worked.   As you've already learned there are people who are really making money with the Organo Gold program, and this is not only those who began the program. Every year there are billions of dollars coming through to this wellness product, and it is a must that you claim your share of this money.

Network marketing is certainly profitable and something that anyone with the desire to succeed with can do, especially with a business that is already as successful as Organo Gold. As you can see the Internet and social media have really changed the way that we do things, and has made it more than possible to get the business you need both locally and globally alike. With such an easier way to do things, you have everything that you need to be successful at your business if you are only willing to make the time to make it work. The Internet will never disappoint you when you want to be successful with Organo Gold, as long as you use all of this information to help you succeed. You can begin to increase your downline, sell more of your product and truly reach the ultimate in success with the help of this information and the wave of the Internet and social media marketing. Local and international marketing are great ways to get all of the people that you want and need involved with your business. If you want to reach your fullest potential you can certainly do it these days, but it takes your commitment to being successful. Are you ready to go there and live the life that you have always wanted to live?

One last word of advice. If Organo Gold is your business choice, play for keeps. You are going to come across others in different networking opportunities, and they will want you to join with them. There is nothing wrong with other companies per se, but if you wish to make REAL life long income, keep your head down, keep to your plan, and tell the Organo Gold story. It's not important that they buy your story, it's important that you don't buy theirs. If you do, you'll end up regretting it.

Further, if you have an Organo Gold product story, or a business testimonial, I'd love to hear about it. Send me a quick email and I'll follow up with you. Maybe you will be in the next edition of this book! Now that would be a help in creating your credibility! See below for more details.

Brian Kelly

A note on testimonials found in this book:

Each person who made these testimonials did so freely. No testimonial was paid for by the author, publisher, or anyone connected to this book. I have edited them for space and readability, but not in any factual way. My researcher collected these testimonials, and FYI, none of the people knew they would be in this book, nor did they have any other connection to this book. There are literally thousands of people who are now leading healthy lives thanks to Organo Gold.

A special and important note:

Even after extensive research, I am always open to more views. If you have an Organo Gold story to tell about how the product has changed your life or health, please send me your story. If you have a business success story, I welcome it too. My publisher will be updating both the Kindle and Paper versions of this book in the future, and your story can be in the book. Email me at Brian.Kelly.Author@outlook.com By sending me your story, you give me the right to publish it. I may edit it for readability.

My research on Organo Gold and those associated with it has made me truly appreciate the amazing opportunity that it provides. It is just in its infancy, here in 2013, and I predict it to become a major dominate contributor to health, wellness and prosperity for those who are smart enough to commit themselves to spreading the word about Organo Gold.

If you enjoyed this book, please leave an honest review on Amazon. Reviews help others find books that interest them, and help authors do a better job in their next book. If you enjoyed this book and have an interest in Organo Gold, leaving a review here can help spread the word about your Organo Gold story. Feel free to add your product story to the review – by putting in your product story as well as the review of the book on Amazon you spread the word about Organo Gold. Put in your full name if you wish, it will be there for your prospects to see when they search you out and consider you as an upline. It builds your social presence.

If you have constructive suggestions, please write to me at the email above.

I wish each and every one of you a full and abundant life – be healthy and wealthy!

Brian.

Something very special for those involved with Organo Gold – David Williams has a new book out that you will want to order and put into practice right away. I read a review copy and know you will want this ASAP.

How to Recruit Doctors into your MLM or Network Marketing team by showing them a NO Warm Market System

http://www.amazon.com/Recruit-Doctors-Network-Marketing-ebook/dp/B00CCPZ7Z4

Where to Find Doctors – It's not where you think

A new source of Doctors (medical) who are not busy

Perfect for the Wellness Industry

No buying Leads

Not working the phone

This book is going to teach you an amazing system to recruit Doctors and an amazing system for you to build a huge, profitable and unstoppable leg under them - without the Doctor using any of their warm market, 'buying leads' or touching the phone!

Full Discloser: This is a short book. It's less than 50 pages long. It contains no fluff or padding. It's direct and to the point. The system contained is worth hundreds of thousands of dollars in sales, and could retire you. Really. Forget the low price of $8.99, forget the number of pages. This book will show you a fool proof system that ANY one can follow to build an unstoppable MLM Network Marketing business by recruiting Doctors. I have made it newbie friendly, but those with experience will take this system and put into practice very quickly.

This book will cover, step by step, and in very detailed and specific language:

How to recruit Doctors

The 'invisible' secret source of Doctors without a practice that are begging for something like what you will be able to show them

How to recruit busy Doctors with a practice and zero time

How to avoid the 'I don't want to go to my contacts/warm market' objection because you will be teaching them a system that requires ZERO warm market

And No 'buying leads'!

How to fill, yes FILL, meeting rooms with prospects all eager to join and try your products

NO conference calls, webinars, websites, Fanpages, autoresponders etc.

This is the full system, from the free ads you will place to the words on the marketing material you will print. This approached is very inexpensive to follow, quick and easy to implement, and very straight forward.

Also included are the phone scripts and person to person scripts you need to use when speaking to the Doctors, their reception-ists, and to use in getting the appointment.

Forget all the 'usual suspects' techniques, this is not about drop-ping off DVDs, inviting them to conference calls, or creating spe-cial 'Doctors only' presentations. Forget all of that, and forget all of your old scripts and ads.

This system works for Doctors and requires NO Warm Market – I know I said that above, but it's very important you know this.

You don't need any paid advertising, Facebook, Internet, Twitter etc., this is all offline, local, and affordable.

No one has taught you this before. Guaranteed.

I'm going to show you where to get Doctors and how to approach them. This book will reveal to you a hidden world of Doctors who are not busy. I am going to share with you this source, give you all the scripts, the ads, the marketing materials, right down to what to say in the low cost marketing material.

This is David's other book, I'll tell you upfront it's not for newbies, if you are not in the market for new scripts, you don't need this book. But if you are looking for more ideas and scripts for building your business, this is unlike any script book you have ever read. For those in Organo Gold, the How to Recruit Doctors book is a must! This script book below is only for the experienced networker.

MLM SCRIPT TREASURY
NOT YOUR USUAL
NETWORK MARKETING PHONE SCRIPTS

DAVID WILLIAMS

MLM Script Treasury: Not Your Usual Network Marketing Phone Scripts

http://www.amazon.com/Treasury-Network-Marketing-Scripts-ebook/dp/B00CKC5F38

By David Williams

Just released!

This book is full of the top pulling, most valuable and very rare MLM phone scripts that have earned their users many hundreds of thousands of dollars.   I will say right now, the material in this book is NOT 'newbie' friendly. These scripts are for pros. If you don't know what you're doing this book is not for you.

-Turn your prospects voice mail into a recruiting machine!   12 scripts which you can customize

-What do I say to make sure my prospects watch's my DVD or online presentation?

-What is a GAP line and why you should use one, and what to say on it.

-How to take your prospects pulse

-Top Tier Phone scripts – rare and valuable – and great to modify for your own phone scripts

-What to say to get your prospect on to a conference call

-How to close your prospect after a conference call – lots of trial closes, hard closes, and objection handlers

-Common objections and how to turn them back into closing questions

I have chosen scripts that I know you will NOT find in other script books for sale, or the free PDFs that float all over the Internet. The scripts contained here are the kind of scripts that only the top leaders in a program have access to and it usually requires some-one to be invited to join their inner team to gain access to them.

This book is full of very hard hitting powerful scripts that have been used by many top prospectors and closers. You can use this book to build your own scripts by modifying what you find here.

-Scripts to get a prospect to commit to a live conference call

-The hardest closing questions from the industry

-Ads that will get your Voice Mail full, and what to say on your Voice Mail screener – lots of screeners and out bound messages

-What to say to your prospect AFTER the conference call

-Voice Scripts to 'wake up the dead' – get your inactive distributors active again

-Starting your own MLM or Team Call? Need a conference call script? – 4 full conference call scripts inside

-Are you a company trainer? Do you do many trainings? Are your people dying on the phone?

If you are a trainer, a serious upline, on your way to being a player, a 'big dog', this book is for you. If you are putting together your own scripts, calls, establishing your own team, or your own network marketing company – invest in this book. Inside this book you will find: hard hitting, hard closing power calls, what to say when you reach a prospects voice mail, screeners, actual company conference calls, GAP line messages and some special bonuses to get your phone ringing plus much, much more. It's all here.

What is in this book can take a serious player to the next level.

This is most definitely an 'insider's book'.

Williams's latest book:

http://www.amazon.com/Autoresponder-Messages-Network-Marketing-ebook/dp/B00D38WD38

This book contains a professionally written email drip campaign of 30 powerful, engaging and entertaining persuasive email/autoresponder messages focused on your prospects 'Financial Woes' and how YOU can help your prospect solve them.

Warning!

If you have been in Network Marketing for any length of time, you probably have accumulated a list of prospects and their email address. However, many of these prospects have entered the 'witness protection program'. In other words, they never call back or reply to your emails. Most people forget about this list, but there is GOLD in it!

Now, you probably have an email system you pay for that is filled with 'canned' autoresponders about your company, or even some generic versions to send to your list. Sometimes this is part of your 'backoffice'.

But, have you read these autoresponders being sent in your name?

They suck.

Here's why:

You have a prospect who is looking to solve THEIR problem, which is lack of money. They need money, income, some light at the end of the tunnel, cash, maybe some dough to save their home... BUT they are NOT shopping for a MLM company, an INDUSTRY, or how long your company has been in business, or even what your product does...NO... they are desperate for a SOLUTION to their problems!

But if all the emails you send out are about 'the company, the timing, the industry…or how someone else is making money – no wonder they don't bother responding to you!

Can you imagine sending emails to starving children with stories about the kids in your family that have so much food… that they're fat? Of course not. So why send emails to financially struggling people about how others are rich?

Your prospect doesn't care about other people's wealth when THEY are broke and in financial pain. In fact, it works the other why. Resentment, suspicion, distrust.

Their mind is on their lack of money and they are worried.

They are awake all night worrying about their debt because they are in financial trouble.

And what? You send them an email about how old your company is?

It's basic marketing folks; offer your prospect a solution to their problem, and relate to them on their terms.

At this point, all your prospect is interested in is finding 'a way to earn money'.

NOTE *** If you are new and have not earned a respectable income, chances are your upline will tell you to borrow someone else's story, but doing that only begs the question from your prospect– 'well, if everyone else is making money in your company, why aren't you?'

Forget that.

So, what is in this book? Do I teach you how to write emails? NO…NO…and NO!!!!

Is this some lessons on basic copy writing for MLM? Heck NO!!!

But let's face it. Most people can't write a note to save their lives, let alone a well-crafted email campaign. Forget learning a skill that will take you years to master – just use expert messages instead!

That's where this book of powerful 'financial woes' autoresponder messages will come to your aid.

Inside are 30 rock solid emails that focus on your prospects financial situation - with engaging humor and playfulness - showing how YOU and your program can help him out of his or her financial mess.

FULL DISCLOUSER – this is a small book – 30 powerful emails. You are not paying for the quantity of words, you are paying for the quality of the message and for getting your phone to ring.

This book contains 30 well-crafted powerfully written emails that and fun and engaging that will suggest and reinforce to your prospect that YOU are the answer to their financial problems using proven psychological and persuasion techniques.

Take these email autoresponder messages and enter them into your backoffice or your email program. Start dripping on your list with these professionally written email messages – each crafted to have your prospect motivated to reach out and call YOU as an answer to their Financial Woes!

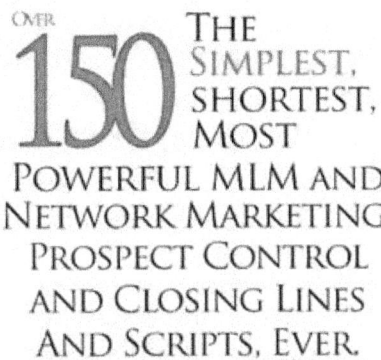

http://www.amazon.com/Network-Marketing-Online-Profes-
sional-ebook/dp/B00DVCTK78

Do you have trouble closing prospects? Do you feel you lose control of your prospecting and follow up calls? Do you have trouble
closing strong prospects – the very ones you desperately want
on your team?

Well, this book is for you. It's the lowest price but highest value
book on Amazon. Why? Because this little book contains over
120 of the strongest, easiest, subtlest closing and 'keeping control' and 'taking control' over the conversation lines for network
marketers.

FULL DISCLOSURE: This is a short book. This book has over 150 'lines'; mostly one line sentences. But don't be fooled by the size of the book. These are powerful closing lines to allow you to close your prospect. This is NOT a book on prospecting, recruiting or even a script book.

This is a book that should be open at your desk as you make your prospecting and follow up calls. If you find you prospect off their script (they never stay on script – only you can do that), these lines will bring you back into control.

They are subtle, but powerful. Here's some samples:

How much does it cost?

Millions of dollars not to get involved

Can you see yourself taking people through a process just like I did with you?

You can't outsource your learning

The table's set

This is thick

I'm not claiming we have an automatic system, I'm demonstrating it

Get into the game with us

Let me layout how the business will start for you

This is just a process to see if there a fit for you

This is not a pressure gig

It's just the way we do this (process)

There's no glory in paying bills

I promise I'm not going to push you, chase you or sell you

I'm not going to come back to close you, but to personalize the business for you

NOTE: with very little modification, you can use many of these lines as ad headers, email subject lines, or as smart and directed text in emails or create new phone scripts or reinvigorate old ones.

Now, you don't have to memorize these lines, you just need to have your Kindle reader, iPad or even your Kindle for PC open, (or you can print out the pages), when you are making your calls. If you lose control of a conversation, or have a strong person on the line (the best kind to recruit), these 'lines' are the arrows in your quiver.

Make these lines your own. They have been collected by professionals and have earned those who have used them millions of dollars, no exaggerating, millions of dollars. Now for .99 cents they are yours.

This book of powerful network marketing closing and control lines provides you with the easiest way to sound strong on the phone. You just need to use them. You need to sound strong. Your prospect will never know what hit them until you are training them, and tell them to pick up this little book.

If they won't spend .99 cents, to get a copy, they aren't worth your time. If they ask you to make them a copy instead, they have just told you they are not worth your time. You now own this book, make these lines your own, become powerful and rich.

You do deserve it!

www.ingramcontent.com/pod-product-compliance
Lightning Source LLC
Chambersburg PA
CBHW051316170526

45166CB00002B/570